Capitalism and Nationalism in Prewar Japan

Capitalism and Nationalism in Prewar Japan

The Ideology of the Business Elite, 1868-1941

Byron K. Marshall

Stanford University Press   Stanford, California 1967

Stanford University Press
Stanford, California
© 1967 by the Board of Trustees of the
Leland Stanford Junior University
Printed in the United States of America
L.C. 67-26528

To my mother and the family

Acknowledgments

One of the greatest pleasures of publishing the results of any research is the opportunity it provides to express publicly one's gratitude to people who have given one aid and encouragement. I should like to acknowledge my great indebtedness to Professor Thomas C. Smith, who first suggested the need for this study and guided my research while I was a doctoral candidate at Stanford University; and to Professors Irimajiri Yoshinaga and Toba Kinichiro of Waseda University, Otsuka Hisao and Nakagawa Keiichiro of Tokyo University, Robert J. Ballon and Sakurabayashi Makoto of Sophia University, and Takeda Kiyoko of International Christian University, as well as to Mr. Paul Kobayashi, for their many kindnesses during my sojourns in Tokyo. I owe a special debt to Kanai Madoka of the Historiographical Institute of Tokyo for his remarkable patience and generosity in guiding me through the intricacies of Japanese historiography. I am indebted also to Professors Richard Lyman, Mark Mancall, Reinhard Bendix, and Solomon Levine, as well as to Gene Tanke, Nancy Donovan, and others at Stanford University Press, who read the manuscript at various stages and offered constructive criticism.

I received indispensable financial support in the form of a National Defense Foreign Language Fellowship, a Foreign

Area Fellowship, and a faculty research grant from the Office of International Programs at the University of Minnesota. (Needless to say, the views expressed herein are my own responsibility.)

Finally, I would be remiss if I did not take this opportunity to express my gratitude to Professor Robert H. Brower for the invaluable encouragement he has given me over the last dozen years.

B.K.M.

Contents

1. *Introduction* 1

2. *Private Entrepreneurs and the Meiji Government* 13

3. *The Meiji Business Elite and the Way of the Warrior* 30

4. *Early Industrialists and the Controversy over Labor Legislation* 51

5. *Business Ideology and the Labor Union Movement* 77

6. *The Japanese Business Elite and the Defense of Capitalism* 94

7. *Conclusion* 113

   Notes 121

   Bibliography 139

   Index 159

Capitalism and Nationalism in Prewar Japan

1. *Introduction*

The ultimate concern of this study of Japanese business ideology is the general problem of social consensus in an industrial society. Man interacts with his fellow men within a context of shared understandings, mutual expectations, and accepted norms—in other words, within the context of a "consensus which relates individuals and groups to each other and provides an integrated body of ideas, beliefs, and value judgments."[1] An essential function of such a consensus is to sanction or legitimize the distribution of power, wealth, and prestige among individuals and groups. In societies the distinction between proper authority and unwarranted domination, between just reward and ill-gotten gain, between the object of respect and the target of resentment, is defined in accordance with this consensus.[2] If the established consensus is to remain meaningful and adequate in periods of rapid and extensive social change, when existing forms of power and wealth are undergoing a redistribution or new forms are being created, alterations or extensions must take place in this network of sentiments and understanding.

The industrial revolution in England was accompanied by the formulation of a new, middle-class social philosophy. This synthesis of ideas from the writings of Locke, Smith, Bentham,

Ricardo, Malthus, Spencer, and others formed the nucleus of the ideology of capitalism in both England and America.[3] The effect of this ideology was to sanction the acquisition of political and economic power by the middle class; to explain why it was just and proper that the leaders of industry and commerce should enjoy an increasingly larger share of wealth and privilege. By providing the basis for a new social consensus, this philosophy of economic individualism, with its emphasis on such themes as the importance of material progress, the virtues of labor and self-help, and the desirability as well as the inevitability of competitive struggle, greatly influenced acceptance of the new social structure that emerged as industrialization took place. Thus industrialization in England and America was accompanied by a restructuring of the value system in order to give a greater prominence to the private entrepreneurs, the "Captains of Industry," who formed the new economic elite.

In Japan also, industrialization produced a new economic elite who, as the leaders of modern business enterprise, were responsible for mobilizing the nation's resources and creating the economic institutions suitable to an industrial society. As in the West, members of this elite individually and collectively acquired a growing share of political and economic power. For the most part, however, the exercise of this power lacked the sort of ideological sanction that served to legitimize the position of the business class in England and America. In Japan, industrialization and its concomitant social changes took place under the sanction of what remained in essence the traditional value system—a preindustrial value system in which there was little provision for the legitimate exercise of power by a private business class. As one student of modern Japanese society put it: "The businessman, even the big businessman, has not yet been able to compete with either the intellectual elite or the government functionary as an ideal type in his culture; and for the practical man, wealth and sheer economic power has not given the general communal prestige or final effective power that political position bestows."[4]

One of the most intriguing aspects of the persistence of traditional values in Japan is the failure of the business elite to promote a new social consensus better suited to support their role in an industrial society based on private enterprise. In their effort to justify a position of wealth and power for the modern business class, Japanese business spokesmen explicitly rejected the major tenets of the Anglo-American capitalist creed in favor of traditional Japanese values. They denounced the Western philosophy of economic individualism for its stress on the pursuit of personal gain, and claimed that Japanese businessmen were motivated by patriotic devotion and a willingness to sacrifice for the common good. Prominent businessmen such as Shibusawa Eiichi went so far as to deny that personal profit was even a consideration in their business decisions. Thus business spokesmen attempted to convince their critics, their workers, and themselves that modern entrepreneurs were entitled to prestige and authority because they served the nation in the same selfless manner as the samurai of old. Nevertheless, the difficulty of reconciling traditional values of group-orientation with the profit-orientation inherent in the institutions of private enterprise served to render the Japanese business elite exceedingly vulnerable to attack from both the socialist left and the ultranationalist right in prewar Japan. In the 1930's, business leaders found themselves faced with the difficulties involved in attempting to justify private ownership and profit incentives while denying any interest in material rewards.

The purpose of this book is to analyze Japanese business ideology in the prewar period in order to explicate this dilemma, and to suggest some of the reasons why the business elite were reluctant to break with the values of the past. I hope to show in particular that their predilection for traditional values arose in large part from the Japanese businessmen's view of their own interests in the early stages of industrialization, and that it was not merely a passive acceptance of an official orthodoxy imposed by political leaders from above. In other words, despite the fact that the interests of the business class would seem to have been poorly served in the long run by a philosophy that stressed the subordination of the individual to the collective goals of the State, it was the business leaders themselves who contributed substantially to both the formulation and the maintenance of the view of society that gained acceptance as orthodox in prewar Japan.

Before proceeding, it would be well to attempt to clarify the concept of business ideology as it is used here. By "business ideology" I mean those ideas expressed by or on behalf of the business class with the manifest intent of creating attitudes favorable to private capitalism.[5] This study, then, is not directly concerned with the origins of the capitalist spirit or the supply of entrepreneurs in Japan, as interesting as those subjects are. Although speculation on the psychological attitudes or personal motivation of individual businessmen may aid us in identifying the factors that shaped Japanese business ideology, our primary concern is with the ideas utilized by business spokesmen to justify the private ownership of industry and to legitimize the authority of the managerial class. (This is not to imply that business ideologies are mere rationalizations adopted out of expediency; on the contrary, I think it quite probable that Japanese business leaders were sincere in their claims about their patriotic motives.[6] Nevertheless, the question of their sincerity is relevant here only insofar as it was raised by critics of Japanese capitalism.) In other words, we are interested in analyzing business ideologies at the overt "phenomenological level." Reinhard Bendix has demonstrated in his studies that this kind of analysis can substantially increase our understanding of class relations in an industrial society;[7] and such an analysis is of particular interest in the case of Japan, for, as Robert Scalapino has argued, the failure of the Japanese business elite to contribute to the formulation of "a philosophy which would give adequate ethical support to the open expression of individual or group interests . . . a theory which would recognize the legitimacy of private interests," was an important factor in the failure of parliamentary democracy in the prewar period.[8]

The Hostile Tradition

The development of business ideology, like the process of industrialization itself, is greatly influenced by social values inherited from the past. The traditional values sanctioning the distribution of wealth, power, and prestige in preindustrial Japan were, on the whole, inimical to the interests of the private business class. Japanese society in the Tokugawa period (1600–1867) was dominated by the military aristocracy—the samurai —which derived its wealth and power ultimately from control over land. Over several centuries a value system had evolved that served to buttress this power and render it legitimate in the eyes of the rest of the population as well as the ruling class itself. Embedded in this value system were norms defining the function and position of the merchant class—norms that were invoked when necessary to justify the subordination of the merchant class to the authority of the samurai elite.

Underlying these values was the widespread acceptance of traditional Confucian assumptions regarding economics and social stratification. The major classes—samurai, peasant, artisan, and merchant—were thought to owe their origins and *raisons d'être* to the separate and distinct functions they performed for society. As the influential seventeenth-century thinker Yamaga Sokō argued:

It was inevitable that class distinctions should arise. In order to live, people must have something to eat. . . . Since farm work cannot be done properly by hand only, agricultural implements must be manufactured . . . and for their manufacture, artisans are necessary. Since manufacturers of articles cannot go about selling their goods to people in distant districts, people to act as intermediaries between the artisans and the consumers of their manufactures become necessary, and these middlemen form the merchant class.

In addition, the requirements of good government necessitated the establishment of a ruling class under whose wise guidance "culture, public morals, and order [could] be maintained throughout the country."[9] In the Chinese view, individual mobility between the functional groups within this organic society was thought desirable if warranted by ability. In the process of adapting Chinese ideals to the realities of Tokugawa society, however, this aspect was ignored or repudiated by Japanese thinkers; the lines between the major classes were considered frozen, and the division of labor was determined by hereditary status.[10]

The justification for the dominant political position of the samurai class was rooted in assumptions about the moral supremacy of the samurai way of life. In the Confucian tradition, good government required a ruling class whose members not only tended to the mechanics of administration but also displayed in their personal conduct the highest human virtues. Chief among these virtues was that of selfless devotion to duty: that is, devotion to the public interests, to the welfare of the State and the people. This was conceived of as being fundamentally opposed to the preoccupation with profit and the calculating concern with private interest that were seen as inherent in the merchant way of life.[11] Since the activities of the merchants were thought to be governed only by self-interest, and their contribution to an agrarian economy was of minor importance, the merchant class was relegated to a social position below even that of the peasantry.

The antagonism felt by samurai officials and moralists toward the merchant class was intensified by the changes that gradually took place in the relative economic position of the samurai and merchant classes, and the challenge these changes posed to the supremacy of the samurai aristocracy.[12] The economic position of the aristocracy had begun to deteriorate by the end of the seventeenth century. Government expenditures and the cost of living for the samurai class as a whole consistently exceeded incoming revenue, and in the course of the eighteenth and early nineteenth centuries the aristocracy fell deeper and deeper into the debt of the urban merchant class. Although contemporary observers disagreed on the best means of solving this problem, there was widespread agreement about the general causes. The majority laid the blame squarely on the head of the wealthy merchants, who had "given free rein to their cleverness and greed," and had "caused prices to go up and down at will, all making huge profits."[13] It was argued that this situation had been brought about by the growth of the use of money and the increase in the level of consumption of the populace as a whole, changes fostered and encouraged by the merchant class for selfish ends.[14]

This economic crisis was perceived as being closely connected to the issue of national morals. The material success of the merchant class set a dangerous example for the other classes in society. Motoori Norinaga, whose heterodox teachings formed the basis for a new intellectual movement in the early nineteenth century, warned that the rise of the merchants was having a demoralizing effect on all classes, and that the people were gradually becoming obsessed by the idea of securing quick profits, and were neglecting their regular pursuits.[15] The effect on the peasantry of exposure to the merchant mentality and to the attractions of urban life was particularly dreaded: "If the farmer communities become contaminated by the habits of merchants, they will come to detest farm work, and will fall into the mistake of regarding agriculture as economically unsound."[16] The influence of the merchants on village life not only endangered the source of tax revenue of the feudal elite but threatened to destroy the traditional virtues of the peasantry, who formerly had been "naturally honest, simple, easily moved by blessings, quick to follow reason, and satisfied with their daily food."

Even more dire consequences were predicted if the spread of mercenary attitudes among the samurai class was not checked. Muro Kyūsō, who served as adviser to the Shogun Yoshimune in the early eighteenth century, wrote that the entire civil administration was being corrupted by the example of merchants lusting after wealth and squandering it on extravagant luxuries.

The "earnest, dependable, hardworking and kind" samurai officials of old, who "had endured hardship as soldiers and had known no luxury even in their dreams," were now extremely rare. Moreover, Kyūsō and other moralists warned, samurai no longer valued the martial virtues or boasted of their willingness to die for their lord. Under the influence of the urban culture of the merchants, the members of the warrior class had come to value comfort more than duty and were no longer fit soldiers, for "if [a samurai] is greedy of money, then you can be sure that he will ultimately be greedy of life. In that case, you should use the blunter word, and say that he is cowardly."[17]

There were thinkers who sought to defend merchants against the charge that they were responsible for undermining the economy and destroying the moral fiber of the nation. Their arguments, however, were not directed at gaining acceptance for merchant values as such, for they did not go beyond the claim that merchants performed an essential function and that commerce need not be an immoral activity. The writers and lecturers of the Shingaku movement, for example, sought to show merchants how to practice the traditional virtues of filial piety, loyalty, and honesty in their daily lives. Members of the Shin sect of Buddhism, which was popular among the famous Omi merchants, claimed that a fair profit was justified; that insofar as the merchant performed a necessary role in the circulation of goods and in the money transactions this entailed, his was an honorable occupation that entitled him to appropriate social and material rewards.[18]

Though such arguments defined a legitimate place for commercial activities within the Tokugawa value system, they could not justify any real change in the social structure or value system itself, nor were they meant to. As Robert Bellah points out, the purpose of these arguments was to persuade others that "the pursuit of trade and industry is a form of loyalty to the realm and thus honorable for the samurai or anyone else."[19] Yet the burden of proof remained on the shoulders of those who chose commerce as a means of serving their society, for no doctrine was developed that could justify for the superior man the pursuit of private gain, or justify for the merchant class a position of political and social leadership. A striking illustration of this can be found in Marius Jansen's account of the Kaientai, the trading and shipping company established by a group of Tosa samurai in the 1860's with the aim of strengthening the financial and military position of their *han* (fief). The enterprise was opposed from the beginning by traditionalists within the *han* government on the grounds that "it was a serious error to sink to the foreigners' level and seek for profits." Although convinced that the pursuit of profit for a good cause was not shameful, the samurai in the Kaientai remained so sensitive about ulterior motives that they drove one of their number to commit suicide to prove he was not motivated by selfish interest.[20] Such extreme cases were doubtless rare, but they typified the ideal view that the samurai were "the most noble of the four [classes of] people" precisely because "being truly pure of heart, they never [sought] their own profit."[21]

Traditional Attitudes in the Meiji Period

The Meiji Restoration of 1868 did not bring any fundamental changes in traditional attitudes toward the merchant class. The overthrow of the shogunate and the dismantling of the old political and social structure were engineered primarily by discontented members of the samurai class who had little interest in sharing power with a merchant class for whom they felt neither affection nor respect. There were some among the merchant class, and especially among the rural entrepreneurs, who may have welcomed the downfall of the shogunate; support from such elements may even have been crucial to the success of the Meiji Restoration. But the Restoration was not in any meaningful sense a middle-class revolution;[22] and furthermore, although the new political elite proved keenly aware of the importance of economic development to the future of Japan, and took immediate steps to remove the existing restrictions on industry and commerce, their policies did not necessarily imply approval of the values of the industrial societies of nineteenth-century England and America. After a brief flirtation with Western social and ethical doctrines, Meiji officials returned to traditional sources for the moral inspiration they believed essential to rapid national progress. This can be seen in the educational system: for example, ethics textbooks dating back to the 1870's, which had been modeled on, or in some instances even directly translated from, those in use in England and the United States, were replaced in the 1890's with texts in which the Confucian principles of individual submission to family, to social superiors, and above all to the State were reasserted.[23]

The Meiji Restoration had two important consequences for the status of the business class. First, the Tokugawa merchant class gained remarkably little in power and prestige from the Restoration. On the contrary, when many of the merchant class proved unwilling or unable to adjust to the demands of foreign trade and modern industry, they became targets for the scorn and abuse of the Meiji reformers. For example, in 1873 Inoue Kaoru and Shibusawa Eiichi, young officials in the Meiji government, announced that they intended to resign from government service in order to devote themselves to business enterprise because they believed the old merchants unfit for the tasks of economic modernization: "Sometimes we hear of a few who are reputed for cleverness, but they turn out to be men who rejoice in corruption, engage in speculation or monopolize profits. The worst of them ruin their business and lose their property by cheating, by fraud, and committing all sorts of dishonesty. Now it would be easier to expect a cock to crow in its eggshell than to see those [types] advance at once to the stage of civilization."[24]

Secondly, the use of Confucian ethical doctrines by the Meiji oligarchy to rally the nation to patriotic efforts and to bolster their own prestige as ministers of the Emperor served to reinforce traditional attitudes toward the pursuit of private gain. Meiji statesmen such as Yamagata Aritomo were convinced that private interests were incompatible with the proper performance of one's duty to the State, and warned that progress could be achieved only if the leaders of the nation were superior men "who would not be corrupted by thoughts of personal gain or fame [and] who would not falter in their public devotion."[25] As a consequence, the profit motive remained highly suspect. Indeed, the charges of ignorance, timidity, and incompetence that were leveled against the traditional types of merchants in the Meiji period were secondary; the more serious accusation was that of selfish and unpatriotic behavior: "Examine the speech, appearance, attitudes, character, spirit, and habits of our merchants—all are shameful. They fight over trivial sums and short-range profits, and their only ambition is to feed themselves and their families. They know nothing of sovereign or country, nor are they concerned with the prosperity of the people or the good of society."[26] The pursuit of private gain by merchants who dealt in exports and imports was particularly condemned. Nishimura Shigeki, a prominent Confucian scholar whose articles frequently appeared in the business magazine *Jitsugyō no Nihon* (*Business Japan*), equated profit seeking in this sphere with treason. Nishimura accused some Japanese merchants of injurious "conspiracies with foreigners," and he warned that immorality would ruin Japan's foreign trade. "Once their hearts have been seduced by the chance of immediate profit," he wrote, "then . . . Japanese merchants will no longer be trusted abroad." To Nishimura, moral rectitude was as essential as business acumen:

In the feudal period, the merchants were placed at the bottom of the four classes, and everyone . . . treated them with contempt. The merchants themselves had no self-respect, and none of them paid any mind to learning or morality. Most of them thought that it was sufficient if, by acting with cunning, they could realize a profit. But the man of commerce is the one who undertakes trade directly with the foreigner. . . . He must be a man of the highest quality and courage, completely different in character from the feudal merchant.[27]

In subsequent chapters we shall examine the persistence of traditional attitudes in the Meiji period in more detail. It is important, however, to emphasize at the outset that the Restoration did not afford the businessman who aspired to a position of honor and authority in Japanese society any relief from the necessity for explaining, justifying, or rationalizing his pursuit of commercial gain.

2. Private Entrepreneurs and the Meiji Government

Vested interest, religious piety, the commitment to "history,"[1] sheer inertia—the psychological barriers to industrialization are as manifold as they are formidable. The core of the powerful ideology that sanctioned the efforts to overcome those barriers and to transform Japanese society in the late nineteenth century was "reactive" nationalism:[2] that is, the appeal to all Japanese to put aside personal, class, and regional differences in order to defend Japan against foreign intrusion. Industrialization, in other words, was advocated first and foremost as a means of avoiding humiliation at the hands of the Western powers. The fact that the Meiji Restoration and the far-reaching changes it set in motion took place in and derived their justification from a sense of national crisis colored all subsequent Japanese political, social, and economic thought. Nationalism played an especially important role in shaping the ideology of the modern Japanese business class, in that it provided a ready-made rationale for government aid to private business, and for the rejection of the doctrines of laissez-faire economics.

Reactive Nationalism and the Industrialization of Japan

From the beginning of the nineteenth century onward, the fear of foreign encroachment grew steadily in Japan. However, by the 1860's the recognition of the superiority of Western military power had served to convince even the most xenophobic of patriots that some degree of intercourse with the foreigner was essential if Japan was to acquire a knowledge of modern military technology.[3] The effects of the opening of foreign trade, moreover, soon led to an awareness that the economic challenge posed by the West was every bit as urgent as the military threat. Trade with the West not only caused serious dislocations in the existing handicraft economy, but also created a need for specie. Since the commercial treaties that Japan had signed with America and the European nations under duress forbade such measures as protective tariffs, the Japanese government had little control over the quantity or type of foreign goods being imported. Japanese leaders were thus faced on the one hand with a massive outflow of specie that undermined the stability of the national currency and the value of government tax revenue fixed in money, and on the other with an influx of foreign goods superior to and less costly than domestic products, which posed a serious threat to the rural handicraft industries and thus to the standard of living of large numbers of the peasantry. Confronted with the problems of a depreciating currency and growing unrest among the peasantry, the new Meiji government moved as quickly as its resources permitted to stimulate industrial development, hoping thus to increase exports and reduce dependency upon imports.[4]

But though military and economic considerations were unquestionably the most compelling reasons put forth by the advocates of rapid industrialization in Japan, military strength and a favorable trade balance were not the only goals of the Meiji reformers. There was a third aspect to the nationalistic reaction to foreign intrusion: i.e., the intense desire of the Japanese leaders to stand on an equal psychological footing with the advanced nations of the West. The material and cultural achievements of late nineteenth-century Europe and America made a profound impression on the increasingly large number of Japanese who traveled abroad. Earlier visitors, the influential Fukuzawa Yukichi in particular, had written vivid accounts of their travels in Europe and America; but even the best-informed traveler was not fully prepared for the sights that greeted him on his first trip abroad. The effects of such experiences on Japanese attitudes toward industrialization are attested to in numerous diaries and autobiographies. According to one biographer, even the able Okubo Toshimichi, who as one of the inner circle of the new government had good reason to feel satisfied with his own accomplishments, came home from Europe in 1873 with an "inferiority complex."* Okubo and others like him were determined to bring "civilization" and "enlightenment" to Japan—a motive as important to them as any military or economic reason for placing their energies in the service of industrial development.

The interplay of these motives can be seen in the careers and thought of many of the pioneers of Japanese industrialization. Inoue Shōzō (1846–1886), a Chōshū loyalist who spent his career in government, was sent to Germany in 1870 to learn military science. Instead, he devoted himself to studying the woolen industry, and after his return he played a leading role in the establishment of the government-owned Senjū Woolen Mill. Of his decision to go into industry he wrote:

I want to make our country the equal of Europe and America. Today even the small children of Japan talk of enriching the country and strengthening the military, and they call for civilization and enlightenment. But there are few men who really have attempted to discover the tree that has brought forth the fruit of civilization and enlighten-

---

* Sidney Devere Brown, pp. 189–90. Okubo is recorded as having told one of his traveling companions, "I had wanted to overthrow the Bakufu and establish the rule of the Emperor. That task being almost complete, [I felt that] we had done our part. But now I am sorely troubled, for having traveled through the West I see that we cannot measure up to a world so advanced." Quoted in Tsuchiya Takao, *Nihon shidōshatachi*, p. 25. Kuroda Kiyotaka, onetime president of the House of Councillors, underwent an even more dramatic conversion to the cause of industrialization. He left for his European tour one of the chief opponents of extensive railroad development. Upon his return, he apologized publicly and became one of its most ardent advocates. See Hirschmeier, *The Origins of Entrepreneurship*, p. 123.

ment in Europe. . . . After having read something of world history
and geography in my search for the source of the wealth, the military
power, the civilization, and the enlightenment of present-day Western
nations, I realized that the source must lie in technology, industry,
commerce, and foreign trade. In order to apply these precepts and
make the nation rich and strong, we must first of all instruct the people about industry. Then we can manufacture a variety of goods and
export them, import those articles we lack, and accumulate wealth
from abroad.[5]

Government Views of Private Enterprise

The story of the extensive measures taken by the Meiji government to promote economic development has been told in detail
elsewhere.[6] Our concern here is with the attitudes the Meiji
business elite expressed regarding government participation and
intervention in the economic sphere. However, in order to
understand the position taken by business leaders on this issue,
it is first necessary to consider how the Meiji political oligarchy
envisioned the economic role of government.

Although the Meiji government rejected in practice the doctrines of the Western laissez-faire economists, government leaders had no desire to repudiate the private enterprise system. On
the contrary, political spokesmen lamented the fact that the
government had been forced to shoulder a burden properly be-
longing to the people. It was only the backwardness of the economy and the immaturity of the people, they claimed, that compelled the government to take action. When in 1874 Okubo
Toshimichi—the key figure in government economic planning
until his death in 1878—submitted an outline of his proposals
for promoting industry, he bemoaned "the weakness of spirit
of the people," and stated that it was the duty of the government to encourage and guide them.[7] Nevertheless, Okubo took
pains to avoid any direct repudiation of either the principles of
private enterprise or the theory of laissez-faire economics. Instead he advanced the argument that economic policies should
fit the level of development of the nation, and pointed out that
in England laissez-faire policies had not been deemed appro-

priate until the economy had reached a fairly high level of development. Only after there was no longer the need for government initiative or protection had England become the champion of laissez-faire and free trade. In Okubo's view, Japan was then at the same stage of development reached by England in the seventeenth and eighteenth centuries, and it was the England of that period, rather than contemporary England, that Japan should take as her model. Implicit in Okubo's statement was the view that once neo-mercantilist policies had propelled Japan well down the path toward industrialization, it would be feasible to adopt, as England had, the philosophy of the Manchester school.*

These views were echoed in the formal proposals for each new venture that the Home Ministry, which Okubo headed, presented to the Council of State (the *Dajōkan*). They were also repeated in the official statements of principle that accompanied public announcement of new undertakings: for example, the March 1876 request by the Home Ministry for approval of its plan to establish a government-operated woolen mill stated, "It is the natural task of the people to undertake such an enterprise," and indicated that the Home Ministry foresaw the time when the woolen mill could be "entrusted to the people."† This emphasis on the temporary character of the government's involvement in the management of industry was repeated frequently by government officials. It is evident that these men wanted it

---

* Okubo had just returned from a lengthy tour of Europe, including Germany, and the terms in which he couched his views suggest strongly that he had been exposed to the ideas of Friedrich List. List's works, however, did not become well known in Japan until the 1880's; see Sumiya Etsuji, *Nihon keizaigaku shi*, pp. 92ff.

† Quoted in Thomas C. Smith, p. 65. Okubo's original thought had been to subsidize Okura Kihachirō, a rising young entrepreneur who was interested in a government contract for manufacturing woolen army uniforms. Okubo said to Okura when they met in Paris in 1872: "Since you are an entrepreneur starting a new venture, there is the possibility of failing, in which case others who subsequently may wish to enter the field would hesitate to do so. The government should therefore aid you, and after the enterprise is well established, it can be sold back to you." Quoted in Iwata, p. 158.

clearly understood by the public that once a venture was "sufficiently developed," private enterprise should "take it over from the government,"[8] and that the government had every intention of eventually transferring the burden to those "among the people" who desired it.[9] Meanwhile, government spokesmen said, the government wished only to "give the people a profitable example"; and they denied that government attempts to establish modern industrial enterprises were in any way efforts to "compete for profit with the people."[10]

Each new government enterprise was thus carefully justified on the grounds that the people were still unable to establish and operate the needed industries themselves, and that therefore the government had no choice but to take the initiative. Failure to do so at a time when "the very existence of the nation was in peril" would mean disaster.[11]

Business Views of the Economic Role of Government

The basic position expressed by the spokesmen of private enterprise on the question of the economic role of government was in complete accord with that of the Meiji political leaders. Indeed, Meiji entrepreneurs were seldom satisfied that the government was as active as it might be. They produced a steady stream of speeches, articles, and petitions aimed at obtaining increased government aid in developing the banking system, expanding transportation facilities, increasing provisions for commercial and technical education, enlarging overseas markets, and so on.

In stressing the need for this aid, business leaders repeatedly referred to the "crisis" that faced the nation, and consistently sought to take advantage of the prevailing mood of reactive nationalism.* For example, in an 1875 petition for a change in the

---

* It should be noted again that we are not here concerned with the ultimate *motives* of the entrepreneurs. Although Meiji businessmen as a group gave every appearance of having been as sincere in their professions of patriotic devotion as any other segment of their society, this is beside the point. What is significant here is the use to which they were able to put patriotic slogans in furthering the development of private business.

regulations governing the formation of commercial companies, Minomura Rizaemon, the chief manager (*bantō*) of the Mitsui enterprises, bolstered his arguments with references to the dangerous drain on the nation's specie holdings and the threat to Japan's sovereign rights posed by the activities of foreign merchants.[12] Godai Tomoatsu, the president of the Osaka Chamber of Commerce (Osaka Shōkō Kaigisho) in 1880 and a leading promoter in that city, told the government that it was impossible to "lay the foundations of wealth and strength" in Japan unless the government increased its efforts to give protection to the businesses run by "the people." Like Okubo, Godai pointed out that laissez-faire economics were not appropriate to Japan's present situation. "Consider the progress of national development in the various countries abroad. Countries like England, America, and France, which are the very models of civilization, prosper today because their governments exerted sufficient effort and protected commerce and industry at the time when these had yet to flourish."[13]

Businessmen expressed even greater concern for the nation's future after the Diet was created in 1890 and the representatives of rural interests who opposed higher land taxes attempted to reduce government spending. If the government did not continue to give special attention to the needs of commerce and industry, business spokesmen warned, the nation would be in grave danger. An editorial in the *Tōyō Keizai Shimpō* (*The Oriental Economist*), for example, called attention to the plight of China as an example of what would befall Japan if the government cut back expenditures for the promotion of industry: "Anti-business attitudes have been an evil in China since ancient times; and despite the wealth of resources in that country, industry has not developed. The fact that China is a weak country ridiculed by the rest of the world is the result of anti-business attitudes."[14] The petitions that business organizations regularly sent to the Diet contained similar warnings. The leaders of the Nagoya Chamber of Commerce, complaining that the existing election rules gave too much weight to rural constituencies, claimed that because the Diet was dominated by agrarian landholders, it continually ignored "problems involving the prosperity of the country's commerce and industry. Truly this is cause for great fear for the future of the nation!"[15] The Osaka Chamber of Commerce, petitioning for increased measures to "encourage and protect the enterprises operated by the people," struck an even more ominous note when it proclaimed that "the very survival of the nation" depended upon "a comparatively great advance [in industry] in a relatively short span of time."[16]

It is hardly surprising to find private entrepreneurs urging the use of state resources to promote business interests. Even the ardent economic individualists of nineteenth-century America usually favored tariff protection, subsidies to vital industries, land grants to railroads, and the like.[17] The more significant question is how business reacted to other forms of government intervention, especially public ownership and management of economic enterprises.

The issue of direct government participation in the management of business enterprises did not cause concern among the Japanese business community until late in the Meiji period.* The absence of serious opposition to the establishment of government enterprises in the 1870's can be easily understood in terms of two interrelated factors. In the first place, government enterprise in the early period was confined largely to areas where no private entrepreneur had yet shown a serious intention or capacity to venture. The majority of the old Tokugawa business class were either too shaken by the rapid turn of events in the early Meiji period to do so, or were quite content to remain within their traditional fields of endeavor. The more progressive entrepreneurs who were to form the new business elite had yet to

---

* A search through the annals of the Chambers of Commerce of Osaka, Nagoya, and Kōchi, and the records of the Tokyo Chamber of Commerce reprinted in Shibusawa, *Shibusawa Eiichi denki shiryō* (hereinafter cited as *SEDS*), failed to uncover any trace of opposition to government-owned enterprises prior to the debate over railroad nationalization discussed below. See also Thomas C. Smith, *Political Change*, pp. 92–95.

attain sufficient experience or size to undertake the Herculean task of creating large-scale modern industries. As already noted, it was the vacuum created by the lack of private capital and experience that drew the government into the field of industrial entrepreneurship. Not until the 1880's, when the government had largely withdrawn from the field by selling the majority of its enterprises, did private investment in the modern industrial sector reach significant proportions; hence government-owned enterprises at no time posed a direct challenge to private business, except in the armament and railroad industries. Therefore, it is not surprising that the issue of private-versus-public enterprise remained largely an academic one in the early decades of the Meiji period.*

Secondly, as we have seen, the economic principles that served as guideposts in the formulation of government policy during these early years did not constitute a threat to private business. Private business leaders apparently believed the government's assurances that it had no desire to encroach permanently upon that sector of the economy which, according to both tradition and the example of Western industrial nations, belonged properly to private enterprise. When announcing the sale of government factories, Matsukata Masayoshi (Okubo's successor as the chief architect of government economic policy) had given the business community more reassurance by stating unequivocally: "The government should never attempt to compete with the people in industry and commerce. It falls within the sphere of government to look after matters of education, armament, and the police, while matters concerning trade and industry fall outside its sphere."[18]

Nevertheless, the question of government ownership of economic enterprises did arise in the 1890's, when a heated debate broke out over the issue of railroad nationalization. In

---

* This is not to deny that there was a great deal of theoretical discussion of the principles of laissez-faire economics. For a survey of the introduction of Western laissez-faire and protectionist doctrines in the 1870's and 1880's, see Sumiya Etsuji, *Nihon keizai gakushi*, pp. 32–150.

1892, Matsukata, then serving as Prime Minister, proposed to the Diet a bill authorizing government purchase of private railroads. Matsukata and the bill's supporters reasoned that private companies could not undertake the expansion of services essential to the rapid growth of the economy, because such expansion would require a huge outlay of capital with little immediate return.[19] The Diet, however, consistently refused to vote the necessary funds until 1906. But the failure of Matsukata's plans was not brought about by business opposition. On the contrary, the nationalization proposal had the active support of the majority of the business community in all three of the nation's economic centers, as was evidenced in the resolutions passed by the Chambers of Commerce of Tokyo, Osaka, and Nagoya.[20] The Tokyo Chamber of Commerce, for instance, agreed that private enterprise lacked the ability to carry out the task of creating an efficient nationwide rail network. Masuda Takashi, who represented the Mitsui firm on the committee that endorsed the original proposal in 1891, stated that although he was not in principle an advocate of government ownership of railroads, he was convinced that the purchase was unavoidable "in view of the prevailing conditions of the economy."[21]

Although the majority of the business community favored nationalization, there were prominent businessmen who disagreed. Shibusawa Eiichi, for one, opposed the plan, but his arguments were not based on opposition to public ownership per se. Shibusawa was concerned rather with the special problem of the influence of the military on the planning of railroad development. He had long argued that decisions on new routes should be made primarily on the basis of economic factors. In his view it would have been detrimental to the economy to give undue weight to the military's concern for inland routes less vulnerable to foreign attack; and he feared that the military would have too great a say if the government were to operate the railways.[22]

A second source of opposition to nationalization was the Mitsubishi Company. Here we find one of the major exceptions to

the generalization that Japanese businessmen shunned arguments based on laissez-faire doctrines. Shōda Heigorō, Mitsubishi's chief executive in Tokyo, skillfully invoked the central
tenets of the classic Anglo-American argument in his fight
against government ownership. In December 1898, for instance,
Shōda told the Railroad Council (Tetsudō Kaigi):

[The advocates of nationalization] argue that there are so many competing lines that profits have shrunk and capital and labor are wasted.
But does there exist any enterprise in which there is not some waste
of capital or labor? The progress of enterprise in this world depends
upon the fact that there are both those who make profits and those
who suffer losses. I say that if we expect enterprises to progress, they
must be left alone—left to natural selection and the survival of the
fittest—without artificial intervention.[23]

In 1908, after the nationalization bill had passed the Diet,
Shōda wrote: "I opposed the nationalization of railways from
the beginning. My reasons were that it confiscated the property
produced by private individuals, thus disregarding the guarantees under the law, and that the result of unification would be
a reduction of competition."[24] Mitsubishi's allies in the Kai-
shintō, the Progressive Party, also opposed nationalization; and
the party's leader, Ōkuma Shigenobu, claimed that he too was
an advocate of laissez-faire economics. Speaking as Minister of
Agriculture and Commerce in 1897, Ōkuma told the press:
"There is much debate about whether the Ministry of Agriculture and Commerce should intervene in business or leave business alone. From the beginning I have agreed with the principle
of laissez-faire, and have been opposed to intervention. Free
competition is very essential to the development of business.
It is necessary to promote a spirit of independence in businessmen."[25] Shimada Saburō, another Diet leader who opposed the
nationalization plan, also invoked the principle of free competition, declaring: "Unless competition continues, all progress in
railroading will cease, for the same reason that it ceases in other
instances."[26]

The majority of business leaders, however, continued to support nationalization on the grounds that economic progress as well as national defense required the early creation of a nation-wide transportation system.[27] In reply to Shōda and the others who opposed government ownership, business leaders who favored nationalization argued that the shortage of investment capital in a country such as Japan, which was still in the early stages of economic development, made government ownership essential. Advocates of laissez-faire, according to Masuda Takashi, simply did not understand this.[28]

The railroad nationalization bill was the only instance in which government ownership gave rise to any serious debate among the business community in the Meiji period. Although an occasional voice was heard calling for the government to limit the scope of the manufacturing enterprises it had retained after 1880,[29] government ownership of economic enterprises other than railroads did not constitute an issue about which the majority of the Meiji business class felt compelled to argue.

The Question of Government Regulation of Business

The support and protection of industries and the development of transportation facilities were not the only forms of intervention practiced by the Meiji government. Two other major types of intervention influenced business attitudes toward the role of government: 1) the regulation of relations between management and labor; and 2) the regulation of competition between private entrepreneurs. The question of labor relations will be treated at length in Chapter 4. The issue of government regulation of competition was of much less importance, and can be summarized briefly here.

The commerce and industry of Tokugawa Japan had been organized for the most part within a tight framework of associations (*nakama*) not unlike the European guilds.[30] Shortly after the Meiji Restoration, these associations were ordered to disband on the grounds that they encouraged monopolistic practices unsuited to the new age: "For the sake of their own private profit [businessmen] form associations to prevent others from entering the same occupation, and this causes prices to

rise. . . . Since today is a time for spreading civilization and
enlightenment, all so-called *nakama* will henceforth be dis-
solved."³¹ The rapid changes following the Restoration, however, brought severe economic dislocations, and it was not long
before some merchants were blaming their difficulties on the
dissolution of the old guilds.³² Mitsui's Minomura Rizaemon,
for example, pointed out to the Council of State in 1875 that
the *nakama* had served to provide essential facilities for credit,
and that the production of exportable goods such as silk and
tea was being hindered by the lack of these facilities.³³ Three
years later, the newly formed Osaka Chamber of Commerce
gave similar reasons for requesting permission to organize *dōgyō kumiai*—literally, "associations of those in the same occupation." The Osaka leaders blamed the business slump in the
city on the decline of cooperation between merchants: "Even
those in the same occupation have no means of mutual assis-
tance, and each man runs after his own profit without regard
for the harm done to the country as a whole. Business is steadily
falling into decline."³⁴ The proposal to create *dōgyō kumiai* to
perform some of the same functions that the old *nakama* had
performed was discussed at length by the Tokyo Chamber of
Commerce in the spring of 1879.³⁵ Opinion was divided. Shibusawa spoke in favor of such associations, saying that they would
promote the mutual benefit of their members and also provide
a basis for closer liaison with the government. Masuda Takashi,
who had taken over the reins of the Mitsui firm when Minomura died in 1877, expressed his fear that government supervision and regulation of commercial associations would result
in "governmental interference in commerce."³⁶ Shibusawa's reply to Masuda illustrates the attitude toward government regulation of competition held by the majority of businessmen as
well as by most government leaders. The question of whether
government intervention is beneficial, said Shibusawa,

is a matter that basically depends upon the degree to which the customs of the people are advanced . . . and should not be discussed in
the abstract. Although free trade is the highest principle in England,
it is not [necessarily] appropriate in other countries. Can there be

any question that in our country at the present time it is to the general good that the guidance of the [economic] system should be entrusted to the government?[37]

Masuda's doubts were not allayed, however, and the Mitsui-controlled *Chūgai Bukka Shimpō* (*Domestic and Foreign Price Reporter*) took the occasion to editorialize on the dangers of relying too heavily on government regulation of competition:

There are those who say that theoretically it is good to leave management alone, yet argue that merchants have nothing to fall back upon and consequently are unable to secure credit and are thus ruined .... What sort of talk is this? Business is opportunity; the thing that merchants should depend upon is their own diligence. If they cease to be diligent they should not have anything to fall back upon. If we build them something to lean upon, they will become indolent.[38]

No further action was taken on the petition to create *dōgyō kumiai* until January 1883, when the Ministry of Agriculture and Commerce asked the Tokyo Chamber of Commerce to discuss the question again. Once again Masuda expressed fear of the "evils of government intervention" and argued that the authorization of such associations by the government in the Tokugawa period had led inevitably to monopolistic practices. Masuda proposed that instead of setting up officially regulated organizations, the government allow legal force to be given to trade agreements between businessmen under existing laws covering private contracts, and argued that matters of trade were properly left to "the self-rule (*jiji*) of those in commerce and industry." Those who favored the *dōgyō kumiai* system, however, replied that private agreements could not be made sufficiently binding to provide an adequate foundation for cooperation between businessmen; and Okura Kihachirō, their leader, argued further that such cooperation was essential if the quality of Japanese exports was to be raised and the nation was to attain its proper position in the sphere of foreign trade.[39] Despite Okura's arguments, the Chamber of Commerce voted to advise the Ministry that the matter was best left to private agreement, and that no special regulations were necessary.

The issue was still not resolved. In the following year (1884) the government instructed the representatives of the Kangyō Shimonkai—the regional committees of businessmen and officials created by the government to advise on economic matters —to discuss the question at their general conference. The type of objections set forth by Masuda apparently carried little weight with those from outside Tokyo who attended the conference, for there was general agreement that competition, if left unchecked, would degenerate into the practice of "harming others to profit one's self."[40] The conference endorsed the *dōgyō kumiai* system; and in November 1884 the government promulgated the Standard Regulations for Occupational Associations (Dōgyo Kumiai Junsoku).[41]

Thus the majority of the Meiji business class accepted not only the principle of restricted competition but also the view expressed by Shibusawa that it was the proper function of the government to enforce such restrictions. Again, as in the case of government management of economic enterprises, those in favor of government intervention used the argument that such intervention was justified by the backward condition of the Japanese economy and the need to meet the economic challenge of the West.

There is one further noteworthy instance of the Meiji government's intervention to control competition. This was occasioned by the famous duel between the Mitsubishi shipping lines and the Kyōdō Un'yū Kaisha (The United Transportation Company), a company that had been formed originally with government support to challenge Mitsubishi's domination of Japan's shipping industry. The struggle between the two companies was the fiercest industrial battle of the period. By 1885, the cutting of shipping rates in the attempt to drive the opposition out of business had pushed both companies deep into the red, and a number of business leaders feared that both would collapse if the duel were to continue. In August 1885 a group led by Okura Kihachirō, one of the most prominent businessmen of the period, asked the Tokyo Chamber of Commerce to appeal to the government to intervene. The petition warned of the harm that would be done to the nation if both of Japan's modern shipping firms were to fall into bankruptcy. Not only would this open the way for foreigners to handle an even larger share of Japanese foreign trade, but it would also undermine the country's military position, since Japan depended on the merchant marine for defense in the event of war.

Mitsubishi's Shōda Heigorō entered a written objection to the petition, taking the position that the government should not be called upon to regulate competition. On the other hand, Shōda claimed, there was not room for two companies in the shipping field; and he suggested that a merger be negotiated between the parties involved. Okura, supported by Shibusawa, opposed the idea of a merger on the grounds that competition was generally desirable, but stated that since unchecked competition might in this case endanger the shipping trade of the nation, the government should supervise the competition between the two companies in order to keep it within reasonable bounds. Shibusawa agreed that since shipping was crucial to the nation's economy, such government supervision could not be said to be "unwarranted interference." Significantly, Shōda, who thirteen years later fought the nationalization of railroads on the grounds that progress demanded competition, based his case for a merger on the plea that "if it is left to the survival of the fittest, the inferior will certainly suffer a crushing defeat."[42]

These examples of the view taken by businessmen of the proper role of government in the economic life of Meiji Japan reveal how little appeal the main tenets of laissez-faire economics had for the majority of private entrepreneurs. The relative absence of expressions of hostility toward government of the sort that pervades the classic Anglo-American business ideology is striking. But this restraint was not simply the result of that fear or sense of inferiority vis-à-vis government officials sometimes attributed to the Meiji businessman;[43] we have seen that Meiji business leaders did not hesitate to openly oppose government policies when they felt it was in their interest to do so.

The chief reason for their willingness to accept intervention was simply that at this time government intervention posed little threat to private business interests. Government leaders were convinced that they must do everything in their power to encourage private enterprise, if the economy was to grow and the nation to become great; and business leaders, for their part, were acutely aware that the fate of individual private enterprises, as well as the expansion of the economy and of business opportunities, depended greatly upon the active participation of the government. Moreover, businessmen were able to take advantage of both the government's commitment to rapid industrialization and the nationalistic temper of the times to obtain the types of intervention most favorable to private business.

Mitsubishi's opposition to railroad nationalization and Mitsui's opposition to the *dōgyō kumiai* clearly demonstrate the ability of Meiji business leaders to seize on lassez-faire principles when they believed government intervention was threatening their interests. The point is that these were simply not the sort of weapons business generally felt the need of, since in most instances the government was firmly on the side of private enterprise. Nevertheless, the willingness of government leaders to support and protect private enterprise was by no means the only reason that Japanese business spokesmen had little recourse to laissez-faire justifications. In order to fully understand the differences between business attitudes toward government in Japan and those in the United States and England, it is necessary to turn to the related problem of the doctrine of economic individualism.

3. The Meiji Business Elite and the Way of the Warrior

Japan's rejection of doctrinaire laissez-faire principles in favor of the more pragmatic views of nineteenth-century economists such as Friedrich List is easily understood in terms of the economic problems that the Meiji government and the Japanese business community faced. These economic considerations do not, however, provide an adequate explanation of the rejection of the central concept of nineteenth-century Western economic thought, the concept of economic individualism.

The view that self-interest is the mainspring of the economic system, and that profit-incentive is the mechanism that keeps this spring wound tight, has long been fundamental to the rationale of the Western private-enterprise system. Though there are other moral and political sanctions for capitalism, its economic justification has depended primarily upon the acceptance of the notion that self-interest is a prerequisite for the initiative, effort, and efficiency necessary for the economic betterment of society. Although Adam Smith's classical concept of the "invisible hand" —the force that guarantees that selfish action will ultimately contribute to the public good[1]—has always been subject to question, the doctrine of the natural harmony of interests has remained a key premise in the defense of private enterprise. As reinterpreted by the Social Darwinists, this doctrine was very much in vogue in the latter half of the nineteenth century, when Japan was first exposed to Western economic and social philosophy.[2] In 1877, for example, the New York *Evening Mail* carried this comment on the death of Cornelius Vanderbilt: "It is part of the Providence that overrules all human efforts and events, that such incarnations of energy as Mr. Vanderbilt *must* serve the public uses, whether they want to do it or not. . . . Men work more wisely than they know, and the making of money cannot go on without promoting the progress of society and multiplying its good opportunities."[3] Several decades later, a professor of Yale University proclaimed with equal faith that "the lowest passions of mankind, ostentation and ambition, petty rivalry, the love of saving, and the love of gain, while they bring their own penalty upon the individual who unduly indulges them, are still overruled for good in their operation upon the interests of society."[4]

The most striking aspect of Japanese business ideology before World War II was the rarity of such declarations of faith concerning the profit motive. Although there was little question regarding the merits of private enterprise, there was a prevalent tendency among Japanese business spokesmen to ignore or repudiate the role of self-interest. In effect, the spokesmen for Japanese capitalism drew a distinction between the operation of private enterprise and the pursuit of private profit, defending the former without attempting to justify the latter.

The Doctrine of Economic Individualism in Japan

Japanese observers were not slow to grasp the essential concepts of the Western doctrine of economic individualism. For example, in 1872 the Iwakura Mission, sent by the government to learn more of Europe and America, reported that "the people of Europe in general live a life of greedy competition. . . . One meaning of the principle of liberty is the pursuit of private profit, and in this sense it is taken as essential to the encouragement and satisfactory progress of productivity."[5] Numerous translations of Western studies in the field of economics appeared in the years immediately following the Restoration, and the ideas of the classical economists soon became quite familiar to literate Japanese. The most influential proponent of the English school was the founder of Keio University, Fukuzawa Yukichi.[6]

Even before the Restoration had opened the floodgates to Western ideas, Fukuzawa was arguing for a new view of the pursuit of commercial gain: "In the primitive, uncivilized world men could not benefit themselves without injuring others; therefore those who were active in mind and body and accomplished things were always thieves. This is not so in the civilized world; those who gain riches and fame always benefit others by doing so."[7] In the three decades between the Restoration and his death in 1901, Fukuzawa produced a steady stream of books and articles, the central theme of which was the importance of individual initiative in building a strong and wealthy nation. He blamed Japan's backwardness primarily upon the Confucian education that had prejudiced Japan's leaders against commerce and the commercial class. At the heart of this prejudice was a scorn for private profit; and in an attempt to correct this bias, Fukuzawa argued for the acceptance of the Western view: "Everyone in the country individually aims at increasing his own private wealth. . . . Desiring more and still more, they utilize all their secret skills in the competition for new things, and in this way new methods are evolved, land is reclaimed and developed, machines are invented, transportation and communications are improved, and the investment of capital is effected."[8] Japan could not become an advanced nation, he claimed, until it was recognized that "private zeal is the source of national wealth," and commercial activity was accorded proper respect.[9]

Other Japanese exponents of economic individualism such as Taguchi Ukichi, the editor of the *Tōkyō Keizai Zasshi* (*The Tokyo Economics Magazine*), were willing to accept the extreme view that self-love and the desire for personal pleasure

were the motivating forces behind all human action.[10] Fukuzawa, however, was less concerned with this type of question
than he was with the problem of how man could best fulfill his
obligations to society and contribute to the advancement of the
nation. He stressed that the individual could only fulfill such
obligations by first creating an economic base for personal independence and self-reliance.[11] It was this element in Fukuzawa's
thought, rather than the emphasis on the ultimate, indirect benefits to society, which appears in the writings of those businessmen who sought to justify private gain. Fujiyama Raita, one of
the many graduates of Keio University who became prominent
business figures, interpreted Fukuzawa's views in the following
manner:

This is the way I felt about entering the business world: . . . the times
were changing, and although there was to be no change in the basic
principle that [our efforts] were for the sake of the nation, the most
important thing to be realized . . . was that our national wealth was
inadequate. We had to advance our material civilization and not
remain behind the countries of the West. . . .
    In order to realize the spirit of Fukuzawa and the motto of Keio
University—"Independence and Self-determination"—we had first
to cultivate ourselves and set our own households in order. Of course,
cultivating oneself and ordering the household are things also advocated by Confucian scholars. The samurai, however, . . . thought that
even to touch money was filthy, and they despised money-making as
something done only by townspeople or peasants. This was erroneous. It becomes possible to strive for the sake of the national
society only after making oneself and one's family completely independent. . . . Our first policy, therefore, was to build a basis for [per-
sonal] independence; then progress from there to creating a wealthy
household, and then to producing wealth for the country.[12]

The Rejection of Economic Individualism

Economic individualism, even the moderate and circumspect
version of it propagated by Fukuzawa, had few articulate advocates among the leaders of the Japanese business world. While
self-reliance, individual initiative, and independent action were
highly praised in Meiji business literature, the profit motive,

competitive pursuit of material goods, and the other elements essential to the dogma of economic individualism as preached in England and the United States were usually deprecated. In their place were professions of patriotic fervor and willingness to sacrifice for the common good, coupled with denials that personal enrichment played a significant role in motivating Japanese entrepreneurs.

The most explicit disavowal of the tenets of economic individualism can be found in the writings of Shibusawa Eiichi, whose long career as the leading banker in Japan and abilities in writing and public speaking made him perhaps the most influential single voice in the Meiji business world.[13] For Shibusawa, the son of a wealthy peasant family, who had been educated in the Confucian tradition, all views of man and his relationship to his society could be resolved into a simple dichotomy between selflessness and selfishness, or the "objective" and the "subjective" views:

There are in the final analysis only two types: i.e., those who consider the existence of self objectively and those who consider it subjectively. The objective view regards society first and the self second. The ego is disregarded to the point where one sacrifices the self for the sake of society without hesitation. The subjective view, on the other hand, is selfishly aware of the existence of the ego in all situations and recognizes the existence of society only secondarily. To this extent it is willing even to sacrifice society for the sake of the self.[14]

Shibusawa had nothing but praise for self-reliance when interpreted as, "Let us do what is ours to do entirely on our own, without the help of others."[15] But he found Fukuzawa's notions of self-reliance and independence too "subjective" and therefore too anti-social to be acceptable. The ultimate consequence of such "subjective" attitudes, he warned, was moral anarchy, since men were neither wise enough nor saintly enough to restrain their acquisitive instincts once they were allowed to indulge them: "We would end in a situation in which the appetites could only be satisfied by men looting from one another. If the human heart comes to that, then the ultimate result would be such indecent behavior as forgetting our benefactors, turning our backs on our friends, and abandoning our loved ones."[16]

Shibusawa thus could not accept the idea of an invisible force that brings good out of individual cupidity. To him, the price of individual competition was too high:

One must beware of the tendency of some to argue that it is through individualism or egoism [*jiko hon'i*] that the State and society can progress most rapidly. They claim that under individualism, each individual competes with the others, and progress results from this competition. But this is to see merely the advantages and ignore the disadvantages, and I cannot support such a theory. Society exists, and a State has been founded. Although people desire to rise to positions of wealth and honor, the social order and the tranquillity of the State will be disrupted if this is done egoistically. Men should not do battle in competition with their fellow men. Therefore, I believe that in order to get along together in society and serve the State, we must by all means abandon this idea of independence and self-reliance and reject egoism completely.[17]

It was the "objective" view that was stressed most often by businessmen in discussing their own motivations and careers. In his rejection of individualism, Morimura Ichizaemon, made a baron for his part in the development of trade with the United States, emphasized the interdependence of men in society. He claimed that he had always felt that his first duty as a businessman was "to act in such a way as to express gratitude for the benefits [*on*]" he had received from society.[18] Kinbara Meizen, another entrepreneur noted for his lofty ideals, declared that he had spent his life in imitation of the devotees of the Ikkō (Single-mindedness) Sect, who meditated constantly upon the Buddha. Kinbara claimed that rather than meditating on the Buddha, he had "planned with singlemindedness for the good of the country."[19]

There are many variations on this theme, but what is of significance here is the pronounced tendency to view service to society in terms of self-denial and sacrifice. Morimura wrote: "Even supposing one tries, and no profit is gained, or one suffers a loss; if it is to the good of the State, then one should continue to try. I state positively that the secret to success in business is the determination to work for the sake of society and of mankind as well as for the future of the nation, even if it means sacrificing oneself."[20] In 1908, in response to an inquiry about a recent failure he had suffered, Suzuki Tōsaburō, a key figure in the development of the Japanese sugar refining industry, summed up his own personal business philosophy:

I am a businessman. I have no interest in dabbling in books or paintings, or in taking my ease in luxurious mansions. My calling [*honbun*] is to run businesses. Even if I lose the capital I have invested in a business, I do not regret it in the slightest, since business [as a whole] has gained. Even if my work should prove unsuccessful, the research will be inherited by those who come after. . . . Once an enterprise has been launched, society ultimately benefits.[21]

In the early 1880's Godai Tomoatsu, the prominent Osaka promoter, had already acquired a sizable fortune. When asked about his future plans, he replied: "It has never been my hope to spend my life in idleness and pleasure. The wealth of the Empire must never be considered a private thing. . . . My hopes will be fulfilled when the happiness of the nation is secured, even if I have failed, and this wealth has disappeared."[22] In the rhetoric of the period, the highest accolades an entrepreneur could receive were, "He did not become a businessman merely for the sake of wealth,"[23] or "Even if his enterprise had proven unprofitable, it would still have benefited the nation."[24] The ideal businessman, as one prominent entrepreneur said of a colleague, "always put himself last and the public first. He took as his single guiding thought service to the national society."[25]

This emphasis on self-sacrifice in the service of the nation permeated even the discussions of the attitudes and qualities that make for success in business. Indeed, according to Hatano Tsurukichi, founder of the Gunze Silk Company, only those who were properly, i.e., altruistically, motivated could expect to achieve success:

Some of those who have been successful in great enterprises . . . may have been motivated in the beginning by greed, or private interests, or personal ambition. But by the time they reached success, they had completely cast off this vulgar type of thinking . . . and thought only of the public good, the benefit of the society and the nation. Although there are some who have been successful without this attitude, it has been by sheer chance.[26]

There was often the implication that an entrepreneur needs in some sense the lofty goal of service to the nation to sustain him in his labors; or as Morimura put it, the man who can overcome adversity and reach success "is the man who has in his breast the great concept of 'nation,' and has resolved never to quit until he drops."[27] The implication was that those who lacked this sense of duty would fail; and, of course, insofar as the definition of success itself includes patriotic service as an essential element, this is tautological. Proponents of such views, however, meant failure in the usual sense of the word. Morimura, for example, went so far as to attribute the collapse of one of his early ventures to the fact that he entered it without a "spirit of dedication" to the good of the country. "I had merely a shallow desire to make a profit. As a result, I was negligent in a number of matters."[28]

These professions of selfless devotion were not limited to statements of abstract principle. The literature is full of references to specific instances when businessmen claimed to have persevered in their ventures despite heavy losses, because they put the public good ahead of personal gain. This common theme can be illustrated by the brief anecdote told of Fujita Densaburō, an important Osaka businessman. In 1897, the Finance Minister, Matsukata Masayoshi, proposed putting Japan's currency on the gold standard, a change highly detrimental to Fujita's banking interests. Fujita immediately sought an interview with the Minister. However, far from attempting to make Matsukata change his mind, Fujita encouraged him to carry out his plan, saying, "If the gold standard is put into effect, my bank will fail. Although as an individual my losses will not be small, yet for the sake of the nation I hope that you will accomplish it."[29]

Though patriotic motives were enough to entitle a businessman to praise, a mere contribution to economic progress was not sufficient to confer prestige. Spokesmen for the Japanese business class made no attempt to defend moral shortcomings in terms of unintended good results. On the contrary, the idea that private vice might on the balance add up to public virtue was emphatically repudiated: "There are in the world certain politicians and businessmen who have rendered great service to the nation, and it is said that therefore their misconduct must be forgiven. But we must realize that if, apart from their meritorious service to the nation, these men cause confusion in public morality and pollute the integrity of youth, then they have committed great wrongs that cannot be atoned for by their meritorious deeds."[30] This view was summed up succinctly by Shibusawa: "To go bankrupt because of moral principle is not to fail, even though it is to go bankrupt. To become rich without moral principle is not to succeed, even though it is to become rich."[31]

None of this, of course, was intended by these Japanese businessmen to imply that they believed all personal gain was immoral. Nevertheless, their position was a rather paradoxical one, for they seem to have been saying that the private businessman is entitled to a profit for himself so long as he does not aim at it—in other words, he deserves material rewards by virtue of his willingness to put the good of the community ahead of private gain. This apparent paradox might have been resolved by a thorough discussion of what constituted just profits or legitimate rewards; but such discussions are not to be found in Meiji business literature. Fukuzawa's argument for the necessity of an economic base for independent action was, as we have seen, reasonably straightforward. Shibusawa's attempts to deal directly with this subject, however, are more typical of the majority, if only because of their ambivalence.

In a discourse entitled "An Explanation of the Harmony between Morality and Economics," Shibusawa argued that the traditional Japanese scorn for profit-making was based on a mistaken interpretation of the Confucian Analects:

[Because] humanity has been prone to seek gain, often forgetting righteousness, the ancient sage, anxious to remedy this abuse, zealously advocated morality on the one hand, and on the other he warned the people of profit unlawfully obtained. The later scholars misunderstood the true idea of their predecessors and made the hasty conclusion that righteousness and gain were incompatible. . . . They little thought that all sorts of industrial work and the existence of cooperative systems are conducted according to certain regulations based on moral reason and mutual confidence. The result is that they came to believe that poverty is clean and wealth unclean.[32]

According to Shibusawa, who resorted to textual exegesis in the effort to prove his point, Confucius really meant to condemn the acquisition of wealth only when it involved wrongdoing.[33] Speaking on this subject in another context, Shibusawa went so far as to suggest that he believed material incentives were necessary to economic progress: "If . . . we pass laws that say that the wealthy must necessarily subsidize the poor, then men will no longer strive after wealth. . . . This would be a great misfortune, because wealth is always increased through intelligence, ability, and the efforts of men."[34]

Although it might appear from these quotations that Shibusawa was on the verge of developing a coherent justification for the acquisition of private wealth based upon a distinction between moral and immoral means, in fact he could not be content to let the matter rest there. Mere adherence to an ethical code in the conduct of business, while necessary, was not sufficient to render the acquisition of wealth legitimate. The accumulation of private property could only be considered justifiable if the individual's goals and motives as well as the means were moral: i.e., if the individual aimed at the enrichment of the nation and the promotion of the general welfare.[35] Nor did Shibusawa stop there. He denied that self-enrichment could even be justified as a secondary motive. He explained to one critic that his own considerable fortune had been acquired, as it were, accidentally:

Business could not be carried on without adequate funds. Hence I bought shares or stocks and received salaries. In this way my fortune increased; but that was not my real purpose. . . . I buy shares with one hundred thousand yen. Times being favorable, they may increase to two hundred thousand or three hundred thousand yen. My object does not lie in the increase of wealth, but from the nature of the business it so happens. That is all. Never for a moment did I aim at my own profit.[36]

Similar professions of altruism and patriotic devotion appear with tedious regularity in the speeches and writings of Meiji businessmen. There was even a great vogue for incorporating such words as *kokueki* (national benefit) and *teikoku* (imperial) into the names of companies and products. As Ronald Dore has remarked with humor, "Match factories and beef butchers all claimed to 'profit the nation,' " and "even the sewerman operated an Imperial Honey Bucket Service."[37] Even to contemporary observers this occasionally appeared somewhat ludicrous. Natsume Sōseki, the celebrated novelist, commented: "When the bean curd man peddles his wares, he is not doing it for the sake of the State. His basic purpose is to gain the means by which to live . . . though indirectly this may benefit the State. . . . But, wouldn't it be awful if he always had to keep that in mind and eat his meals for the State, wash his face for the State, and go to the toilet for the State."[38] Yet it is extremely rare to find any hint that Meiji businessmen found the posture uncomfortable. Only occasional exceptions can be cited. The author of an article offering general advice to management, obviously feeling that the trend had gone too far, was compelled to remark: "The objective of commerce is making a profit. There is nothing shameful in stating this. . . . Insofar as the good of the State is involved, it is as a consequence; what should be aimed for is profit."[39] The suggestion of a more significant rebellion against restrictions on the expression of private interest is contained in an interview with Hatano Shōgorō, then a director of the Mitsui Bank. Hatano, a graduate of Keio University and a former journalist on Fukuzawa's newspaper *Jiji Shimpō*, deplored the reluctance of Japanese of all classes to openly defend their own economic interests, and pointed admiringly to the manner in which self-interest was accepted as a legitimate motive in politics in the United States.[40] If we assume that other Japanese businessmen felt similar frustrations, how can we account for their reticence?

The Search for Status

Part of the reason why the doctrine of economic individualism failed to take root in Japan lies in the fact that many of the men in positions of leadership in the Meiji business community were former samurai.* As Ronald Dore has pointed out, such men, educated in the tradition of devotion to duty, often "recoiled from a way of life the avowed end of which was not fulfillment of status-defined duty or the performance of honorable deeds, but the accumulation of material wealth."[41] This was true not only of those who had spent their early youth within the Tokugawa cultural milieu but also of their sons, who grew to manhood after the Restoration, since classic Confucian concepts and traditional Japanese values continued to occupy an important place in the education of Japanese youth despite the importation of Western learning in the Meiji period. Thus, to cite one example, Matsukata Kojirō (1865–1950), the son of the Meiji statesman Masayoshi and president of the Kawasaki Shipbuilding Company from 1896 to 1928, had this to say of his first reaction to the world of private business: "I recall that when I first went to Osaka to enter the business world I was annoyed by the continual bowing and scraping. . . . I felt as if I were bowing [to

---

* One sample of 50 leading entrepreneurs active between 1868 and 1895 lists 23, or 46 per cent, with samurai backgrounds. If we include the sons of wealthy peasants, many of whom, like Shibusawa, had received a Confucian education, the figure is increased to 36, or 72 per cent (Hirschmeier, pp. 248–49). See also Sakata Yoshio, "Shikon shōsai ron to shizoku shusshin jitsugyōka" ("Samurai Spirit and Commercial Talent, and Businessmen of Samurai Origin"), in *Jimbun Gakuhō*, XIX (1964), 1–28; and Thomas C. Smith, "Landlords' Sons in the Business Elite," in *Economic Development and Cultural Change*, IX, 1, Part II (October 1960), 93–107.

money]. Although I could endure it, I felt it was inhuman to bow down to money."*

Whatever the true inner feelings of such men—and we should not assume that such statements were necessarily insincere—there is no question that they were under considerable pressure to rationalize their motives for entering private business. The need to explain their decision to others, if not to themselves, is frequently indicated in the literature. Kaneko Kentarō, a high-ranking government expert on financial matters, tells a story that illustrates this point. Kaneko recalls his initial indignation when in the late 1870's his friend Hara Rokurō decided on a career in banking rather than one in government. Kaneko and Hara had become close friends during their years as students in the United States, and in their enthusiasm for building a new Japan they had sworn an oath to each other that they would "devote themselves to the good of the State." Hara returned home first, and when Kaneko arrived sometime later, "there was Hara the samurai wholly engrossed in making money at the bank." Kaneko berated him for having broken his oath. "If all he had intended was to become a mere shopkeeper or take up a trade, there was no need for him to have gone abroad to study."[42] When Godai Tomoatsu, the Osaka promoter, left the government in 1869, he too was called upon to defend himself against the charge that he was abandoning his duty to the nation. He wrote a friend to reassure him on this point: "Although I have left my post, I was born in this country and it is never out of my thoughts. . . . Please set your mind at ease; it is still my intention to serve the country."[43]

This pressure to justify their business activities accounts in part for the enormous emphasis placed on "service" by the Meiji

* Asano and Asano, p. 23. Hirao Hachisaburō, Matsukata's successor as president of the Kawasaki Shipbuilding Company, recalled that in the 1880's the students at the Tokyo Higher School of Commerce were embarrassed to wear the school badge in public, and that when the badge was redesigned and an image of the god Mercury took the place of the word "commerce," student morale improved considerably (Kawai Tetsuo, p. 52).

businessmen. When Matsukata Kojirō confided his misgivings about commerce to another samurai who had entered business, the latter reacted violently: "His face flushed and he cried angrily, 'What! Is it not for the sake of the State that we undertake these enterprises? What is painful about bowing for the State?' "[44]

Claims that one was working primarily "for the sake of the State" become more understandable when placed in this context. But Meiji business spokesmen were not seeking merely to persuade others that private business was an honorable occupation. Their repeated references to the role played by businessmen in promoting the national welfare can also be viewed as part of an attempt to elevate the status of businessmen for political reasons. Despite the extent to which the proponents of industrialization had succeeded in identifying the survival of the nation with the need for economic growth, Meiji business leaders were still far from being satisfied with the limited political influence the business class was accorded. In the 1890's, groups of prominent businessmen launched the first of a series of campaigns aimed at increasing the political status of the business class; and Meiji business ideology must be viewed in the light of these campaigns.*

Prior to 1890, Japanese government and politics were dominated by a small group of men who had come to power with the Restoration, and business interests were served primarily through connections with members of this ruling circle.[45] With the establishment of the Diet in 1890, however, it was no longer

---

* Scalapino has written at length on the question of business participation in politics: see esp. pp. 246–93. I feel, however, that he has based his discussion too heavily on the complaints by business leaders that the response of the business community was inadequate, and has overemphasized the reluctance of Meiji businessmen to enter the political arena. There is no question that the campaigns to increase the political influence of the business class through greater representation in the Diet met with only limited success, and that this fact was of great importance in explaining why businessmen resorted to covert means to achieve their political ends. Nevertheless, business spokesmen did put considerable effort into the drive to enhance their public image, and it was this political need that helped to shape Meiji business ideology.

possible for business leaders to rely upon personal connections alone, and they responded by taking steps to insure that business interests would also be represented in the Diet. At least two business clubs were formed prior to 1890 primarily to discuss political matters,[46] and in 1892 a conference was held to plan a nationwide organization to encourage and assist in the election of businessmen to the Diet.[47] These early efforts did not meet with great success, largely because the election laws were heavily weighted in favor of rural taxpayers. Hence, in the four elections held between 1890 and 1895, the number of representatives from the business class at no time exceeded 38—less than 13 per cent of the Lower House.[48] After the Sino-Japanese War, however, new efforts were made to increase that number, including a campaign to revise the election laws. Editorials in two new, pro-business magazines, the *Jitsugyō no Nihon* (*Business Japan*) and the *Tōyō Keizai Shimpō* (*The Oriental Economist*), repeatedly argued that the Diet could not be expected to reach intelligent decisions regarding economic problems unless business was properly represented. Just before the 1898 election, for example, an editorial in the *Jitsugyō no Nihon* stated:

It has been nine years since the opening of the Imperial Diet, and elections have been held four times during this period. How many representatives are businessmen? They still do not total more than a tenth of the Diet; and of those who call themselves businessmen, many are merely self-proclaimed businessmen who neither take part in business enterprises nor have any experience or knowledge of business. . . . Although the relationship between business and government is closest in matters involving fiscal planning, taxation, and the construction of the means of communication and transportation, a connection exists in almost all spheres. . . . Yet there are no [sic] Diet members who really represent the businessman. Moreover, the ordinary representatives lack experience and knowledge about business, and the result is that there is a tendency toward empty theorizing.[49]

As suggested in the editorial, the chief target for criticism was government fiscal policy, especially the size of the military budget on the one hand, and the relative proportion of government tax revenue from agriculture and business on the other. In December 1898 businessmen from Tokyo, Osaka, Yokohama, and Kyoto gathered to organize the League for the Increase of the Land Tax (Chisō Zōcho Kisei Dōmeikai). Shibusawa addressed the meeting, calling for an expansion of the political power of the business class:

How lamentable it is when we men of commerce and industry compare [our situation] with that [of the businessmen] of America and Europe. Truly we are still in our infancy. Before the Restoration, the merchants and artisans—those whom we call businessmen [*jitsu-gyōka*] today—were shunned and considered the lowest of the four classes in society. But business enterprise has advanced since then, and today . . . the country cannot progress further in such circumstances.[50]

Shibusawa's estimate of the situation was echoed by other leading businessmen. In an article contributed to the *Jitsugyō no Nihon,* Mitsui's Masuda Takashi complained bitterly that although people had come to understand the importance of commercial and industrial undertakings, they still refused to acknowledge properly the contribution made by the men who found and guide such enterprises: "In recent years those who advocate raising the nation through commerce and industry have steadily increased in number, and agrarianism [*nōhon-shugi*], it would appear, has been repudiated. Nevertheless, if you consider how things really are in our country, you can see that it has not changed since pre-Restoration days. The men of commerce and industry . . . are not the equal of other classes in social prestige."[51] What irritated Masuda most, as it did Shibusawa, was the inability of the business community to exert what he felt was its proper influence in the political arena: "Power in this society is monopolized by the politicians, and men of commerce and industry have hardly any share in it. Although you would think that even a half-grown child would laugh at anyone who said that artisans and merchants should be placed beneath the samurai and the peasants, in fact even educated men have not yet completely cast off these feudal ideas."[52] The revisions in the election laws in 1900 gave increased political power to the urban population, but business spokesmen were still not satisfied that the suspicion cast upon the activities of the merchant class by the Tokugawa moralists had been substantially lifted. "They urge building the country on the foundation of commerce and industry," Okura Kihachirō told a business club after the 1902 elections, "but in actuality they do not give commerce and industry proper weight."[53]

The major theme in this campaign to remove the stigma from business and to give proper weight to commerce and industry was not that the businessman deserved a place above that of the samurai, but that the businessman himself was a reincarnation of the feudal warrior.

The Businessman as Warrior

In their quest for greater social recognition and political status, the spokesmen for the Meiji business class sought to create a new image for the men who ran Japan's modern enterprises. No attempt was made to rehabilitate the image of the Tokugawa commercial class. Instead, the modern entrepreneur was portrayed as a member of a different species. In contrast to the old merchant, ignorant, vulgar, grasping, and immoral, the new businessman was pictured as the embodiment of honor, propriety, and the other virtues practiced by those who follow *bushidō* (the way of the warrior) and the Confucian ethic. The Meiji "Captains of Industry," it was claimed, were hardly distinguishable from the pre-Restoration "men of high purpose"— the *shishi* who had plotted the overthrow of the Bakufu shogunate, or the legendary samurai heroes of earlier feudal periods. Indeed, the most striking feature of this image was the degree to which it incorporated the feudal ideals that Fukuzawa, Shibusawa, Masuda and others sought to change. In essence it was not so much a forging of a new image as a recasting of the old one to permit the inclusion of warriors whose weapon was the abacus rather than the sword.

The primary distinction drawn between these new "men of

affairs" (*jitsugyōka*) and the old shopkeepers (*sūchōnin*) lay not in their technical knowledge, which received only secondary mention, but in their moral superiority and patriotic fervor.[54] Whereas the traditional merchant was represented as acting out of greed, the modern entrepreneur was said to be motivated chiefly by his desire to serve the nation. In this context, service to the nation meant contributing to the building of a rich country and a strong military. The extent to which the contribution of the business elite was discussed in the military idiom is noteworthy. The military in Japan had always enjoyed great prestige, and this had recently been further enhanced by the victories over China and Russia. It was hardly surprising, then, that businessmen should attempt to raise their own status by claiming that their contribution to the nation's welfare was of a similar nature to that of the fighting man. Businessmen exhorted one another to greater efforts "in the competition of foreign trade, which is peacetime war,"[55] and business journals editorialized on the need to "battle the Europeans for commercial supremacy in Asia."[56] Commencement Day speakers told business school graduates that they must seek to aid the nation through foreign trade rather than domestic;[57] and they were urged to go abroad to study foreign markets "like troops secretly reconnoitering the enemy's positions."[58] Okura Kihachirō was praised as "that brilliant general of the commercial wars,"[59] and Shibusawa was compared to the eleventh-century patriot Minamoto Yoshie: "Just as the samurai gathered behind Minamoto to follow him into the battle of war, so now the younger generation gathers around Shibusawa to follow him into the battle of enterprise."[60]

Such statements were not intended to be mere rhetoric. They were part of the effort to give the Meiji entrepreneur a new look by wrapping him in the cloak of the warrior. The first issue of Inukai Tsuyoshi's economic journal *Tōkai Keizai Shimpō*, a magazine closely associated with the Mitsubishi interests, compared Meiji entrepreneurs to the "men of high purpose" of the 1860's:

A decade or so ago we had in Japan those who advocated expelling
the barbarians. . . . Today, a decade later, there is still no disagreement. . . . There is only one difference: those who wished to expel
the barbarians of earlier times viewed the foreigners as animals and
attempted to drive them away by force of arms alone. By contrast,
we today view the foreigner as basically a man and an equal, and we
attempt to fight him with economics—to do battle by means of
trade.[61]

After dismissing the traditional merchant type as useless in this
struggle, Inukai climaxed his article with a plea to the ex-
samurai: "Oh, you men of high purpose [*shishi*]—having been
born in Imperial Japan during this age, you want our commercial
fortunes to prosper and our national strength to be extended.
Let us unite our hearts, pool our strength, and together support
this great effort!"[62] Many ex-samurai did come to occupy key
positions in important business firms, and much was made of
this fact. Just after the Sino-Japanese War, the *Tōyō Keizai
Shimpō* claimed:

At present, samurai and those who have received a samurai education are in charge of, and make up the staff in, Mitsui, Mitsubishi, the
Yūsen Kaisha, the Bank of Japan, the [Yokohama] Specie Bank, the
railroad companies, and the other large firms. Look at the leaders of
our business world—are not the majority of them samurai who have
been educated in *bushidō*? Although a few are not, an examination
of their conduct and character will reveal that none of them are without respect for honor, integrity, and fidelity to their word. Respect
for these things is the true meaning of *bushidō*.[63]

Individual businessmen were equally anxious to drive this point
home. Hara Rokurō's response to the accusation quoted earlier,
that he had forsaken his duty to serve the nation by leaving
government service, is typical: "After all, from the point of view
of rendering service to the country, is there really any difference . . . between taking part in the government as an official
and enriching the nation by devoting one's efforts to business?"[64]
Kinbara Meizen was even more emphatic in his denial that military men alone could perform patriotic deeds: "*Hōkō* [service]

does not merely mean the lifelong determination of a samurai to give up his life at the feet of his lord. The first principle of *hōkō* lies in keeping the family enterprise in order, fulfilling one's vocation [*honbun*] as part of the nation, and above all else, devoting the mind and exhausting the body to the utmost for the sake of the State."[65] To illustrate the same point, Morimura Ichizaemon told a story of how, as a young clothier, he had been approached by a samurai who wished a garment made from a piece of silk. The silk had been given to the samurai by his lord, and on it were written the words "*jinchū hōkoku*"— "Utter Loyalty in Service to the Country." This, we are told, greatly inspired Morimura: "The man, in other words, had resolved that when the time came he would put on [the garment] and sacrifice his life for his country. . . . I was deeply moved, and felt that this was not merely the way to behave in battle; it was the way one should conduct himself in business too."[66]

The primary point of contrast between the classic Anglo-American capitalist creed and the ideology of the Meiji entrepreneur lay in the manner in which the two sought to assert the right of the business elite to social and political influence. The Anglo-American creed glorified business itself, claiming that participation in the world of economic competition bred leadership of a type not found in other occupations: "In this fierce though voiceless contest, a special type of manhood is developed, characterized by vitality, energy, concentration, skill in combining numerous forces for an end, and great foresight into the consequences of social events."[67] Meiji business ideology, on the contrary, seldom attempted to glorify private economic pursuits per se. There was no attempt to reinterpret the role of Japanese business classes of past ages and very little attempt to establish the modern businessman as an ideal cultural type. The Meiji entrepreneur's claim to a position of leadership in his society was not asserted on the grounds that he had proven his ability by his success in the economic wars. There was no identification of the acquisition of wealth with personal merit, nor was wealth regarded as the yardstick of business success.

Rather, the claim of the Meiji business leader was that he had demonstrated his sincere concern for the defense of the nation by undertaking the arduous task of developing an economic base for national greatness, thereby proving himself as worthy a successor to the mantle of leadership of the Tokugawa samurai as those who served in the military or government. Thus the feudal warrior remained the ideal cultural type even in the ideology of the Meiji business elite, and consequently there was little room for the philosophy of economic individualism that characterized capitalism in the West.

4. *Early Industrialists and the Controversy over Labor Legislation*

We have seen how the nature of the Meiji Restoration, the climate of reactive nationalism, and the economic role of the Meiji government influenced the development of Meiji business ideology. In order to form a clear picture of the course of this development it is necessary to investigate another aspect of industrialization in Meiji Japan, namely the controversy over labor legislation.

It is important to note the degree to which the Japanese, as latecomers to industrialization, were aware of the experience of those Western societies that preceded Japan down the path of industrialization. On the one hand, this example shaped the goals of the Meiji leaders and provided them with the technology to advance toward those goals. On the other hand, the experience of the West had great influence on the formation of Japanese attitudes toward the social problems engendered by industrialization. In particular, the ideological conflict over labor legislation was substantially colored by a knowledge of the social turmoil caused in other societies by industrial revolution. Both Japanese businessmen and government leaders were aware that economic change is fraught with danger, and they shared the hope that Japan could avoid the difficulties Western nations had experienced in dealing with labor problems.

As a consequence, the controversy concerning labor usually centered on the question of the extent to which Western precedents were applicable to Japan. This meant that the industrialist often found himself faced with the choice of denying the validity of Western precedents or accepting government intervention of a kind he considered highly detrimental. As a result, the pressure on Japanese businessmen to seek solutions within their own tradition rather than in foreign ideologies increased.

The Demand for Labor Legislation

The Meiji business community was first confronted in the early 1880's with the issue of government intervention in the sphere of labor relations. In 1880 the Ministry of Finance asked the Tokyo Chamber of Commerce to advise it on the problem of enforcing labor contracts. The Ministry gave as the reason for its request concern over the growing numbers of apprentices and workmen who were induced by offers from rival employers or by opportunities in new industries to leave without fulfilling the terms of their contracts.[1] Opinion among the members of the Chamber of Commerce was divided on the matter. Okura Kihachirō, for one, expressed concern over the erosion of the traditional ties between employers and employees—the loss of "those beautiful customs" under which, according to Okura, masters had treated their apprentices kindly, and the workers in their turn "never forgot their debt of gratitude [*ongi*] to their superiors." Although Okura and a number of others sought legal measures to prevent employees from leaving their masters, the majority of businessmen were wary of government intervention in this area. They were of the opinion that the problem of contract violations by workmen could best be handled by stricter enforcement of existing contract laws, and that no special government action was necessary.

In 1884 the government once again raised the issue of labor laws, this time proposing to define and delimit legal rights and obligations in general, in the manner in which these were codified in the West.[2] In addition to seeking the reaction of the

Chambers of Commerce in the large cities, the government also submitted the question to a conference of representatives from the regional Kangyō Shimonkai (Councils for the Promotion of Industry).[3] Opinion among the business community remained divided over the best means of dealing with the problem of labor contracts, but there was uniform opposition to the suggestion that Japan should adopt labor laws patterned on those of the West. The committee created by the Tokyo Chamber of Commerce to study the matter reported that although industrialists "earnestly desired" the government to formulate laws to "prevent evils," they felt that these laws should not be modeled on the "strict" laws of the more advanced countries.[4] The argument used to support this position was one destined to be invoked again and again in subsequent debates on labor legislation: since the level of development of Japanese industry is still far below that of Europe or America, it is too early to consider adopting the type of labor laws that exist in the West.

The question of labor legislation became a serious issue in the 1890's when the Ministry of Agriculture and Commerce began pressing for a comprehensive statute to regulate working conditions in the growing number of private factories.[5] In August 1891 the Ministry circulated to the various Chambers of Commerce the draft of a law aimed at enforcing minimum health and safety standards and limiting the working hours of women and children employed in factories. The ultimate purpose of such a law, the preface stated, was "to ensure forever the mutual benefit of both capital and labor by protecting the rights of both, and making relations between employer and worker harmonious."[6] Opposition from business circles induced the Ministry to undertake further study and revision of the draft, and not until after the Sino-Japanese War did the Ministry renew its efforts to win approval for a factory law.

In 1896 the government called the first in a series of national conferences to discuss the status of Japan's economy.[7] The revised draft of the factory law occupied an important place on the agenda, and in the long debate that followed the government delegation made its position quite clear. The overriding concern was the need to ensure the peace and harmony within industry that was essential to continued economic development; and the specter of disruptive strikes and social unrest was repeatedly invoked in the effort to persuade business leaders to accept legislation. Again and again the officials of the Ministry of Agriculture and Commerce pointed to the experiences of Western countries and argued, "Unless the State intervenes in some degree in the relations between employer and employee, there is no means of protecting the interests of the employees, and hence there will arise social evils, disturbances, and social disorder. Other countries have suffered greatly from such ills. . . . Today the advanced countries have recognized the need for factory regulations . . . and have enacted the appropriate laws."[8] They did not necessarily challenge the claim of business representatives that conditions in Japanese factories were on the whole very good.* But regardless of present conditions, the bureaucrats insisted, there was still the immediate need "to create the laws necessary to maintain *in the future* the balance between capital and labor, and harmonious relations between employers and employees, thereby protecting *in advance* against any disorders" (italics mine).[9] The government delegates were willing to concede that labor disputes were still rare in Japan, and argued thus: "As the use of machinery grows steadily more intensive and as we pass into the stage of so-called open competition between individuals, there will be a struggle for profits; then we can no longer be confident that the spirit of compassion will prevail among the people."[10]

Their guiding assumption, based upon observation of industrial relations in the West, was that industrialization inevitably altered the attitudes of labor and management, breaking down ties of sentiment and the "spirit of compassion" and giving rise to

---

* See, e.g., the claims by Shibusawa Eiichi and the Sumitomo executive Hirose Saihei, SEDS, pp. 517–23 *passim.* It should be noted that this was still several years before a series of official and private investigations revealed shocking facts about working conditions in Japanese factories. See Okochi, *Labor in Modern Japan,* pp. 6–20.

a relationship based on contractual obligations—a "cash relationship," as one official called it[11]—a relationship fraught with potential conflict. This remained the key premise in the arguments of those who supported the 1911 Factory Act and similar laws that followed it.[12] Other reasons were set forth, including concern for the health of the skilled labor force so essential to economic development, and the moral duty of protecting the weak from exploitation.* But as important as these may have been, the main theme continued to be the fear of class strife such as that taking place in the countries of the West. This point was perhaps put most succinctly by Kaneko Kentarō, then Vice-Minister of Agriculture and Commerce, when he told the delegates to the 1896 conference: "The advantage of being one of those who follow is that it gives one the opportunity to take note of the history of those who have gone before, and to avoid taking the same path."[13]

The Defense of Tradition

Faced with this line of reasoning, Japanese business spokesmen who opposed factory legislation responded with three major objections: (1) the demands for Western-style labor laws were premature; (2) the lessons of Western history were not relevant to Japan; and (3) competition with the West necessitated special sacrifices from all those in industry, i.e., from labor as well as management.

The earliest defense against government intervention in the sphere of labor relations was the claim that such intervention was premature. Here the same premise employed by those who urged government aid and protection for private enterprise was

---

* See SEDS, XXIII, 511–12; Kazahaya, pp. 118–21; and Kishimoto, pp. 81–83. Prof. Okochi Kazuo has singled out the fear of "the deterioration of [the health of] the country's labor power" and the dangerous consequences this would have for Japan's position in international trade as the key motive behind the passage of the 1911 Factory Act; see *Labor in Modern Japan*, pp. 18–19. This was doubtless a factor, but the question of class strife and the effect it would have on economic development would appear to have been the more significant issue in the long debate over government intervention.

used against the adoption of labor laws modeled on those of the West: since Japan is only at the threshold of industrialization, it is wrong to take the institutions of the most advanced nations as models; economic policies must be in accord with the current stage of economic development. As Shibusawa Eiichi phrased it later, "England was in the nineteenth century, but Japan . . . was still in the eighteenth."[14]

This argument was used by the Tokyo Chamber of Commerce when in 1884 it pointed out that there were but a few large factories in Japan: "Consequently the evils have not yet spread as they have in the countries of Europe and America." The representatives at the Conference on the Promotion of Industry held in that year agreed that it was too early to consider enacting the type of laws that governed labor relations in the West. One businessman from Fukui Prefecture argued that Japanese workers could not yet be expected to understand questions concerning "[legal] rights and obligations."[15]

The business leaders at the 1896 Conference on Agriculture, Commerce, and Industry also avoided challenging the principles expressed in the government proposals, relying instead upon the argument that the time was not yet ripe to consider the problem of labor legislation. Masuda Takashi, for example, treated the whole question as one that could be reduced to a simple disagreement over timing: "The subject has been fairly well exhausted. Some argue that laws are necessary [now]. . . . Others say that in the present circumstances they are not necessary, . . . [because] considering the conditions existing today, it is still too early to enact them."[16]

Japanese industrialists and their spokesmen continued to use this argument even after the first stirrings of serious dissatisfaction among Japanese workers had become evident. Dan Takuma, the young head of the Mitsui mining enterprises, who was to become one of the most influential figures in Japanese business before being cut down by a right-wing assassin in 1932, referred to the rash of labor disputes that marked the second half of 1897 as "an infectious disease . . . spreading into all regions." But Dan denied that there was cause for real anxiety: "The development of industry in our country has yet to reach the stage where large-scale strikes develop."[17]

Nevertheless, after the Sino-Japanese War of 1894–95 it became increasingly more difficult to argue that labor unrest was a problem that need not be dealt with until some future stage of economic development. Labor disputes were definitely no longer a rarity, and critics of various political stripe, made more sensitive by their knowledge of social movements in the West, were quick to seize on these incidents as evidence of the need for government intervention.[18] As the number and seriousness of labor disputes increased in the late 1890's and the first decade of the twentieth century, there was gradual shift away from the "too early" position, and a second theme became more prominent as a defense against progressive social legislation. In essence, this second type of argument consisted of a denial of the assumption that industrial relations must develop along the same lines in Japan as they had in the West. By the late 1890's, business spokesmen who opposed factory legislation were placing heavy emphasis on what they claimed were unique to Japanese labor relations—the special feelings of affection and loyalty that traditionally had governed dealings between employers and employees. Men like Dan Takuma were confident not only that it was still too early to become alarmed about the "infectious disease" of strikes, but moreover that the special nature of the ties between employer and employee in Japan could serve as a permanent prophylactic against a true epidemic.[19] They argued, in other words, that Japan's cultural heritage could be used to make her immune to the social diseases endemic to the Western nations.

The exact nature of the traditional tie between employer and employee was not defined very clearly, but there was little if any disagreement on its major attributes: it was a relationship of affection, harmony, and loyalty. The Tokyo Chamber of Commerce described the affection as essentially an extension of familial sentiments: "In our country, relations between employers and employees are just like those within a family. The young and old help one another and consult together in both good times and bad, and they are enveloped in a mist of affectionate feelings."[20] The Nagoya Chamber of Commerce emphasized harmony: "The relationship is a harmonious one, with warm sentiments on both sides, and is the same as that between master and retainer or teacher and pupil."[21] Soeda Jūichi, president of the semigovernmental Kōgyō (Industrial) Bank in 1908, saw a somewhat different parallel: "The master—the capitalist—is loving toward those below, and takes tender care of them, while the employee—the worker—respects those above and will sacrifice himself to his work. The spirit of loyalty and love of country . . . is by no means limited to the relationship between the sovereign and subject."[22] Loyalty and the willingness to sacrifice were also prominent in the views offered by Tamura Masanori, head of the Shimano Spinning Mills: "From ancient times in our country there have been warm feelings [*onjō*] between employer and employee. It has been a relationship similar to that between the [feudal] lord and his retainer. The lord treats the retainer just like one of his own children. The retainer, besides performing his duties in return for his sustenance, has every intention of giving up his life [for his lord] without regret if the occasion should arise."[23]

The crucial point in most discussions was the contrast drawn between this indigenous ethic and the norms of the workplace in Western countries. The Nagoya Chamber of Commerce, for example, pointed out what it thought was one essential difference: "The situation in our country naturally differs from that in Europe and America. The relationship between employer and employee in the countries of Europe and America is generally nothing more than an exchange of labor and money."[24] Others stressed the claim that Japanese capitalists were more "compassionate, warmhearted and sympathetic" than their Western counterparts.[25] Soeda Jūichi doubted whether Westerners could understand the depth of these feelings: "The capitalists of our country have a warm affection for their workers such as Eu-

ropeans and Americans are incapable even of imagining. . . .
Nothing like these beautiful customs can be found within the
capitalist system, or in the labor unions of Europe and America,
which have developed from the ancient institution of slavery."[26]
One opponent of the 1910 Factory Law took the floor of the Diet
to argue that factory laws had been needed in Europe only because European factory managers treated their workers like
animals. Since Japanese management was "very humane" in its
treatment of the work force, he said, there was as yet no sign of
"conflict" or "animosity" on the part of the workers, nor was there
any reason to fear it in the future.[27]

There was nothing novel in this praise of traditional virtues;
Meiji businessmen appear to have been conscious from the first
of the advantages of preserving the time-honored paternalistic
relation between worker and employer. But in early discussions
of this, businessmen tended to accept the assumption that the
highly personal relationships of the past would become increasingly rarer as industrialization progressed. We have already seen
how in the mid-1880's Okura Kihachirō and others had come to
the conclusion that the erosion of traditional ties had reached
the point where legal measures were necessary to prevent workers from migrating from job to job. Although the consensus at
the 1884 Conference on the Promotion of Industry was opposed
to special government intervention, the delegates also noted bitterly the growing tendency for workers to forget their obligations in their desire for higher paying jobs.[28]

By the late 1890's, however, the contrast between Japanese
and Western labor relations was treated as more than merely a
matter of timing. The weakening of the traditional personal ties
between employers and workers was considered not as a necessary concomitant of industrial growth but as a phenomenon de-
pending at least in part upon the types of labor laws the government chose to adopt. Thus in 1898 the Tokyo Chamber of
Commerce stressed that the traditional work ethic need not be
restricted to older forms of business enterprises, but could and
should be maintained in modern, large-scale industries: "Even

in factories that employ hundreds of workers it is extremely rare [to find a case where] workers have rebelled because of cruel treatment by their employer. Truly this is [because of] the beautiful customs characteristic of our country. We must not fail to preserve these beautiful customs permanently. Why recklessly make laws and forcibly interfere in the relations beween employer and employee?"[29] Advocates of factory legislation were repeatedly assured that the traditional family-like ties and sentiments could be sustained "even where hundreds or thousands of factory workers were employed."[30] According to Tamura Masanori, even the great economic change that had taken place by 1910 had not altered the situation: "These beautiful customs are still very much in existence today. Even in the companies and factories where the master-retainer relationship seems weakest, these customs are being perpetuated, and employees have the attitude that they are working for a man rather than for money." Industrialists claimed that, contrary to what their opponents believed, the adoption of Western-style labor laws would prove far more corrosive to harmonious interaction between labor and management than increases in mechanization or the size of industry:

The situation is entirely different here from what it is in those countries where rights and obligations are set by law. To create laws hastily without realizing this fact would, in short, destroy our beautiful national customs and create a people who are cold-hearted and without feelings. If the workers confront the factory managers with coldness, the factory managers will be unable to feel warmth. Ultimately the two will be in constant conflict over matters of wages and hours.[31]

The same point was made in 1898 by the leaders of the Nagoya business community with regard to welfare benefits: "If these [welfare benefits] are now suddenly to be regulated by laws and ordinances and made a question of legal right, then we cannot but fear that the old habits of harmony and cooperation will be destroyed; and as a consequence quarrels will break out and the industrial world will be thrown into chaos."[32]

In reply to those who felt that government regulation of working conditions would prevent Japan from suffering the tragic conflicts that had accompanied industrialization in the West, Japanese business spokesmen developed the argument that the imitation of Western labor legislation would actually serve to foment unrest rather than prevent it. The choice by businessmen of this particular position was dictated in part by the premises on which their critics based their demands for legislation. Only by denying the relevance of Western solutions could Japanese management attack the key assumption that Japan must either learn from the mistakes of the West or inevitably repeat them. But the choice to stress the traditional was dictated by more than mere logical considerations. There were at least two other factors.

The first was the strong conservative tide that had swept over Japan during the late 1880's. In the 1870's and early 1880's, European ideas had enjoyed an astonishing popularity, but this excessive Westernization had led to a conservative reaction and a reassertion of traditional moral precepts in government and education. A growing concern with Japan's cultural heritage was reflected in the 1889 Constitution, the Imperial Rescript on Education of 1890, and the revision of the 1892 Civil Code, as well as in the publications of numerous intellectual groups dedicated to preserving traditional values. Central to this conservative reaction was a vital interest in those institutions that were "uniquely Japanese"—or at least "Oriental"—as opposed to what was Western; and a great deal of attention was given to the traditional norms for interpersonal relations, especially relations within the family.[33] In view of this, it is not surprising to find business groups extolling the extension of familial practices to the workplace. By defending the concepts of interpersonal relations basic to Confucian morality and accusing the advocates of factory legislation of wishing to destroy the revered institutions of Japanese society, business spokesmen were in a position to take advantage of the strong conservative tide in their fight against government intervention.[34]

The emergence of a small but militant socialist movement in

the 1900's gave further impetus to this conservative trend. The threat of direct revolutionary action posed by the socialists had the effect of strengthening the case for preserving traditional norms in labor relations, for businessmen could identify their own views with those of such influential government leaders as Itō Hirobumi, who wrote: "In industry . . . in spite of the recent enormous developments of manufactures in our country, our laborers have not yet degenerated into spiritless machines and toiling beasts. There still survives the bond of patron and protégé between them and the capitalist employers. *It is the moral and emotional factor which will, in the future, form a healthy barrier against the threatening advance of socialistic ideas* (italics mine).[35] Businessmen had reason to believe that by adopting this position, and tarring their opponents with the charge that they were overzealous imitators of foreign ways, they stood to gain support from those segments of the populace who opposed the wholesale importation of Western culture.

The debate over government intervention was only one facet of the broader problem of labor. A second aspect of the problem was the need of management to develop appeals that would make the newly recruited industrial work force respond obediently and efficiently to the tasks demanded of them.[36] Here, as in the debate over factory legislation, Japanese business leaders rejected the types of appeals developed in the West in favor of traditional and "uniquely Japanese" values.

Paternalism in Japanese Management

In English-language studies, the ideology and practice of Japanese labor management is commonly characterized as "paternalistic."[37] Japanese businessmen typically referred to their labor policies as *kazoku shugi* (familism) or *onjō shugi* (affectionism). These terms point to the key element in the Meiji approach to labor management—the appeal for a personal and diffuse relationship between labor and management modeled on that of the cooperative family unit. In the opinions expressed in opposition to the adoption of Western-type labor laws, Japanese business leaders rejected the view that industrial relations must of necessity be determined entirely by the pressures of supply and demand or restricted to a simple exchange of labor for wages. Instead they proclaimed their concern for the worker's general well-being, not simply for his performance on the job. Such responsibility was specifically rejected by management in Europe and America.[38]

We have seen the ways in which the controversy over factory legislation stimulated Meiji business spokesmen to lay stress in public debate on the value of traditional paternalism. It is now necessary to consider some of the reasons why Japanese entrepreneurs may have found it economically rational or expedient in practice as well as ideologically desirable to adopt paternalism as the guiding principle in labor management. In order to explain fully why management found this approach to labor relations attractive in practice as well as in theory it would be necessary to examine in detail the specific circumstances that existed in individual enterprises, for there is evidence that the nature of paternalistic practices varied considerably in different types of enterprises at different stages in their development.[39] Nevertheless, it is still possible to note several general factors and to cite some examples of how these influenced managerial attitudes toward the problem of labor relations as a whole in the Meiji period.

Certainly one of most important of these was the fact that the bulk of Japan's new labor force was drawn from the rural sector of society. This meant that the great majority of the new workers had grown up in agrarian villages where economic, social, and political forces combined to perpetuate traditional attitudes of loyalty and group solidarity, and ingrained habits of respect and obedience to superiors. The character of Japanese farming, with its need for intensive labor and the cooperative development and utilization of water and other communal resources, led to a natural emphasis on group solidarity both within the family and among the family units that constituted the village. The new labor force was thus well prepared to respond to an ideology that stressed the subordination of individual interests to the good of the group, particularly since it was claimed that the group was modeled on the cooperative family.[40] Many workers, notably the young females in the textile mills, cannot be considered ever really to have left the village environment, since they were recruited through family heads and came to the cities with the intention of staying only a few years before returning home. Other workers entered the factories only in order to supplement their incomes during the slack periods when their labor was not needed in agriculture, and thus they moved back and forth regularly between factory and farm.[41]

A second factor affecting managerial attitudes in this period was the small size of industrial plants. In 1882, the average number of workers per private factory was thirty.[42] In 1914, the average figure for all factories employing five or more operatives was only thirty.[43] The point is equally apparent if we consider the total number of manufacturing plants that employed a hundred or more workers. In 1909, for instance, only 1,062 factories employed as many as a hundred workers, and only 58 had as many as a thousand employees.[44] Over a third of the 629,000 industrial workers employed in factories with ten or more operatives in 1909 worked in places with less than a hundred employees.[45] These figures indicate the degree to which face-to-face relations between workers and the managerial staff remained possible throughout the Meiji period.* In such an environment it was possible to preserve a highly personal relationship between superior and subordinate.[46]

A third factor was the extremely high percentage of women workers in Meiji factories, the result of the central position

* The importance of such relatively small factories in the Meiji economy is illustrated by the case of the Oji Paper Company, an enterprise Shibusawa was fond of citing as a model of good labor practices. In 1897, with a labor force of only 363 factory workers, the company produced 32 per cent of all Western-style paper made in Japan. As late as 1907, the Oji plant employed only 739 production workers, of whom almost a third were women (Hazama, pp. 154–56).

occupied by the textile industry in Japan's early industrialization. In 1882, at the beginning of the growth of private enterprise, the textile industry alone accounted for over half of all private factories and approximately three-fourths of factory workers.[47] Of the 45,623 textile workers, only 4,510 were males over the age of fifteen. Although the proportion of textile workers in the total industrial labor force fell as other types of industries came to occupy a more prominent position in the Japanese economy, the proportion of female workers remained exceedingly high throughout the Meiji period. According to one source, the average percentage of women in private factories employing ten or more workers, in the five years 1900–4, was 62 per cent; in the period from 1910 to 1914, the figure was 71 per cent.[48] The high percentage of women in factory jobs was conducive to paternalistic labor policies in at least two ways. On the one hand, the need to persuade family heads to permit their daughters to come from the farms to the cities led companies to provide dormitory housing and other paternalistic benefits.[49] On the other hand, Japanese women, long accustomed to obeying family heads and to playing a subordinate role in society in general, were if anything even more responsive than male workers to appeals for obedience and diligence couched in traditional language.

When these three factors—the small number of workers in the average plant, the large proportion of women, and the village background of the labor force as a whole—are considered together, it becomes possible to understand why Japanese managers confidently expected—and received—a positive response to ideological appeals that stressed traditional norms in relations between superior and subordinate.

A further consideration impelled industrialists to perpetuate the paternalistic approach. This was the shortage of skilled labor that plagued many important Japanese enterprises in the early stages of industrialization.[50] The spinning industry, the first modern industry to be organized on a large scale by private entrepreneurs, felt the effects of this shortage very early. In the 1880's, the cotton spinners in the Osaka-Kyoto area found themselves in fierce competition for an adequate supply of trained workers. In 1888, the firms in this region attempted to solve their mutual problem by banding together to form the Japan Cotton Spinners' Association (Nihon Menshi Bōseki Dōgyō Rengōkai). The members agreed to refrain from conducting raids on the labor of other members, to blacklist troublesome workers, and to arrange for the loan of workers when extra hands were needed.[51] Similar problems motivated the Nagano Prefecture silk industrialists who organized the Federation of Filatures (Seishi Dōmei) in 1902.[52]

Such agreements worked imperfectly, however, and some mills, notably the large Kanegafuchi Spinning Mills, preferred to rely on superior working conditions to attract and hold employees.[53] Asabuki Eiji, a protégé of Fukuzawa Yukichi recruited by Mitsui to run the new Kanegafuchi mills, made frequent rounds of the plant to oversee working conditions personally. It is said that he paid particular attention to details such as the quality of food served in the company cafeteria, where he regularly took his own meals.* His successor, Mutō Sanji, devised other methods to keep the workers contented. Mutō pioneered the practice of making contributions in lieu of personal bonuses to special welfare funds from which only long-time workers could benefit. One Mitsui official explained that such methods were the only way to hold workers; higher

---

* Onishi, *Asabuki Eiji*, pp. 193ff. The head of Mitsui's mining enterprises, Dan Takuma, also insisted that regular rounds by managers helped to maintain morale and to strengthen the bond between management and employees (Ko Dan Danshaku Denki Hensan Iinkai, I, 445). In making this remark, Dan commented that he had been impressed by the sense of intimacy he had observed in the relations between supervisors and workers in England. It is somewhat ironical, in view of the stress on the uniqueness of the Japanese tradition of paternalism, that Japanese managers sometimes admitted that they drew on foreign models when instituting welfare facilities; see, for example, Mutō, pp. 151–56. Even Shibusawa Eiichi used the examples of the Krupp Company and the Waltham Watch Company in discussing the ideology of familism in industry (Obata, p. 167).

wages would only lead to higher bids by competitors. Mitsui was convinced that it was cheaper to institute complex insurance and pension plans than to let wages be determined by supply and demand.[54] The maintenance of company dormitories, a paternalistic practice particularly widespread in the textile industry, not only served to induce young farm girls to come to the city but also made it much easier for the mills to run night shifts.[55]

Spinning mills were not the only type of enterprise in which the problem of recruiting proved conducive to the adoption of paternalistic labor practices. The mining industry is a case in point: the opening or expansion of mines in remote areas posed special labor problems that often favored paternalistic solutions. This statement by Furukawa Ichibe, the founder of Japan's largest copper and silver mining company, exemplifies the manner in which employers proclaimed their willingness to rise to the challenge of providing for the physical and even the spiritual well-being of their workers: "It is exactly like creating a colony. Since the mines are far back in the mountains, a new town or village must be built, with hospitals for public health, schools for education, relief measures for charity, and temples to encourage religious faith among the miners and employees. ... One must attend to all the things that human beings need in this world."[56]

The case of the Furukawa Company also illustrates another way in which paternalistic practices spread. As the more successful Meiji firms grew, they developed into *zaibatsu*, or "combines" of enterprises of various types under a single holding company. Paternalistic practices adopted to meet circumstances in one type of workplace were sometimes extended to other types of enterprises within the same *zaibatsu* firm. Thus when Furukawa built a copper refinery at Nikko in 1906, the new manager, Yamaguchi Kisaburō, persuaded the company to extend the paternalistic philosophy developed in the mines to workers at the new plant. Yamaguchi formed a consumer cooperative and organized a mutual benefit society with contributions from the company to provide aid to workers in the event of personal calamity. He also introduced the practice of sponsoring annual outings for the families of his workers. The purpose of such practices, he explained, was to foster a spirit of cooperation and solidarity.[57]

The problem of recruiting and holding workers was especially serious in those industries that most required sophisticated skills. Since the machinery for a new industrial plant was often imported from abroad, factory jobs frequently demanded skills all but unknown in Japan. There was therefore a need for on-the-job training, and consequently emphasis was placed on binding trained workers to the firm on a permanent basis when possible. At the same time, the demands of the more technically advanced industries forced management to abandon the traditional practice of relying on master craftsmen or subcontractors to recruit, train, and supervise workers. Such subcontractors, or *oyakata*, could no longer be depended upon to train workers in the kinds of new skills needed in modern industries. Moreover, once a worker was trained, it was impractical to tolerate the continued existence of an intermediary who might be tempted to "sell" him to a higher bidder.[58] In many cases the strength of tradition and the desirability of preventing labor turnover combined to produce a system in which many of the paternalistic functions of the *oyakata* were transferred to supervisors at the lower echelon of the management hierarchy. Thus, though the new group leaders were company men who derived their authority primarily from their position within the company hierarchy, they were encouraged to maintain a close and highly personal relationship with the workers under their supervision, to whom they often advanced funds and gave personal advice.[59] It was this type of relationship to which the head of the Shimano Spinning Mills was referring when, in giving his reasons for opposing the 1911 Factory Law, he stated: "Employees feel that they are working for a man rather than merely for money. Their superior often gives them food, clothing, and cash from his own pocket in addition to the wages from the company."*

The shortage of skilled labor in the Meiji period also led management to take an active interest in the general education of workers.[60] The Mitsubishi Company, for example, created a school for the employees of its Nagasaki shipyards in 1899.[61] Other firms, such as the Iwasaki Shipyards and the Shibaura Electric Works, hired young workers and then paid them while they furthered their education in public schools.[62] Although arguments for such practices could be made on the basis of economic rationality, these educational programs, like the dormitories in the spinning mills, were usually held up as evidence of management's general concern for the worker's well-being, and were included in the category of paternalistic benevolence.

In the years following the Russo-Japanese War many companies created educational programs, mutual aid societies, and other welfare facilities for workers. The pressures of the campaign for government supervision of factory conditions, the violent labor disputes during 1906 and 1907, the increasing radicalism of the socialist movement, and the need to ensure an adequate supply of skilled labor in a period of rapid industrialization all contributed to this trend toward paternalism.[63] The spread of paternalistic practices was accompanied by the formulation of an ideological appeal aimed at securing the cooperation and loyalty of Japanese workers.

The Appeal for Loyalty and Diligence

The Japanese approach to the problem of labor commitment was derived from and at the same time served to reinforce the

---

* Quoted in Kanda, p. 5. At least one authority on industrial problems argued that the provision of housing, instruction on family budgets, and similar practices were necessary because Japanese workers were in the habit of squandering their wages on drink rather than providing for their families; see the article by Teshima Seiichi, the principal of the Tokyo Higher School of Industry, in *Tōyō Keizai Shimpō*, October 5, 1905, pp. 1288–89; however, this view that members of the lower class lacked the intelligence to handle their private lives was seldom expressed in the literature on the subject.

general ideology of the Meiji business class. The key theme in the appeal for obedience and effort on the part of employees was loyalty to the collective enterprise and thereby to the Japanese nation. The incentives that management offered in return were defined less in terms of monetary rewards and opportunities for upward mobility than in terms of lifelong security and recognition of the importance of even the humblest work to the good of the enterprise and thus ultimately to the good of society.[64]

Just as Meiji entrepreneurs repeatedly stressed service to the nation in discussions of their own motives, so they called upon their subordinates to think in terms of collective rather than personal success.* The preface to the company rules of the Furukawa mining enterprises, for example, specifically cautioned employees against private greed and admonished them to always remember that the company had been established "for the purpose of repaying [our] debt to the nation [*koku'on ni hōzuru*]."[65] The obligation of labor as well as management to repay the debt owed to society was also stressed by Suzuki Tōsaburō, a prominent figure in the sugar industry. Suzuki urged his workers to practice the teachings of Ninomiya Sontoku (1787–1865), a Tokugawa moralist who became famous for preaching to the peasantry the importance of diligence and frugality as a means of showing gratitude for the benefits received from society and

* It should be noted that most of the following exhortations are drawn from remarks directed to white-collar workers. This point is of some importance in view of the fact that most companies in the Meiji period drew a sharp distinction between office or supervisory staff (*shokuin*) and production workers (*kōin*), and it was not until the 1920's that the most significant features of Japanese paternalism—lifelong employment, seniority wage scales, and family allowances—were fully extended to include employees in the *kōin* category (see below, Chapter 5). The question thus arises whether there were in the earlier period corresponding distinctions made at the ideological level as well. Actually it is not easy to document the content of ideological appeals made to production workers. There are indications that managers did place importance on inculcating proper attitudes in *kōin* as well as *shokuin* employees in the earlier period, but lectures and speeches to production workers were seldom recorded or preserved. Nevertheless, what evidence there is would indicate that the central values in the ideological appeals to production workers did not differ substantially from those stressed in appeals to white-collar employees, despite the differences in practice.

one's ancestors.[66] Hirao Hachisaburō, a former principal of the Kobe Higher Commercial School who served as a top executive in a number of large firms before and after the First World War, was particularly fond of lecturing his workers on the concept of loyalty to the Emperor and the Japanese nation.[67] In commending a subordinate for his efforts in repairing flood damage at the Besshi Mine, the chief executive of the Sumitomo Copper Mining Company urged him on with this reminder: "This great wealth does not belong to the House [of Sumitomo] alone; in larger terms, this wealth belongs to the country."[68]

Success for those in the lower ranks of the hierarchy, as for those at the top, was to be thought of in terms of contribution, and discussions of ambition were usually carefully hedged with warnings against selfish motives. Thus a former president of the Japan Industrial Bank lectured on the values of humility and self-denial to youths who sought success in business, explaining that the key to success was "the determination to distinguish oneself through dedication to the future of the nation."[69] The principal of the Tokyo Higher Commercial School, who later pursued a successful career in banking before becoming Vice-Minister of Education, warned specifically against thinking in terms of material rewards: "The purpose of business lies in the promotion of the public welfare and the good of society. . . . It must not be forgotten that success is not to be measured in terms of personal wealth."[70] Yasuda Zenjirō, the founder of the Yasuda *zaibatsu,* said that legitimate ambition was not the desire to surpass other men, but the desire "to do excellent things better than other men. . . . When a boy or a man comes to me for the first time I tell him simply that . . . if he is coming to work for me, he must be diligent. I give all my employees three rules: they must be sincerely devoted, they must do their job faithfully, and they must leave success to the natural order of things."[71]

The relationship of ability to success was usually discussed in terms of moral qualities rather than innate talent or acquired skills. Shibusawa, in a discourse entitled "Qualities Required in Bank and Company Employees," emphasized the fact that learn-

ing and technical skills were useless without spiritual cultivation (*seishin no shūyō*). He listed the seven personal traits that
he looked for when hiring: (1) honesty (*jitchoku*); (2) diligence and frugality (*seirei, kinken*); (3) trustworthiness (*cha-
kujitsu*); (4) vigor (*kappatsu*); (5) gentleness and amiability
(*onryō*); (6) respect for rules; and (7) perseverance. It should
be noted that neither initiative, self-reliance, ambition, nor intelligence were included. Indeed, Shibusawa cautioned particularly against hiring young men who might turn out to be too
clever or cunning: "I prefer young men without guile, who are
always amiable, loyal, and unpretentious; . . . who are pure and
honest, yet of an active disposition."[72]

Loyalty implied more than passive obedience; it also meant
the obligation of active cooperation in the collective enterprise.
One of the most ardent advocates of "familism" in industrial enterprises was Gotō Shimpei. Gotō, a physician and public health
official who served as the top civilian administrator in Taiwan
from 1898 to 1906, was not himself a private businessman; but
as Minister of Communications from 1908 to 1911 he took an active part in the management of the newly nationalized railways,
and his labor management policies served as models for private
companies.[73] Gotō made frequent speeches to his workers in
which he expounded the virtues of harmony and cooperation:

I preach that all railroad workers should help and encourage one
another as though they were members of one family. A family should
follow the orders of the family head and, in doing what he expects
of them, always act for the honor and benefit of the family. . . . I attempt to foster among my 90,000 employees the idea of self-sacri-
ficing devotion to their work. I also preach the principle of loving
trust [*shin'ai shugi*]. I teach them that they should face things and
other men with love and trust.

Gotō, like his counterparts in private industry, stressed the organic unity of an enterprise: "I also explain the relationship of
each part to the whole, and attempt to make those in the lower
ranks conscious of how essential the connection is between their
jobs and the progress of the enterprise as a whole."[74] Nakahashi

Tokugorō, head of the Osaka Shipping Company, also put harmony and cooperation first on the list of values. He told his employees "[I hope] that you will undertake your duties united in a spirit of cooperation and harmonious friendship. . . . Truly this is the first principle of management and the key to the prosperity [of an enterprise]."[75]

Harmony and cooperation were often discussed as if they were ends in themselves; but the ultimate justification for the appeals for devotion to the progress and prosperity of the enterprise was the need to compete with the West. This was also the justification put forth by management to explain why, if they accepted responsibility for the welfare of their workers, they were opposed to the adoption of higher standards for working conditions.

The Economic Defense against Factory Legislation

Meiji business spokesmen based their economic objections to Western standards for working conditions on the claim that by increasing overhead costs while reducing working hours, such standards would seriously handicap Japan's attempts to compete with the industrial nations of the West. Fukuzawa Yukichi, in his widely read book *Jitsugyōron* (A Discourse on Enterprise), wrote in 1893 that Japan's major hope for competing with English industry lay in the fact that Japanese mills could run twenty-four hours a day.[76] At the 1896 Conference on Agriculture, Commerce, and Industry, Okura Kihachirō expressed the views of many when he said: "The country's production cannot increase unless we sell our various goods cheaply [abroad]. Given this situation, and in view of the fact that there are not sufficient people [skilled workers], we should not deliberately take pains to create such factory laws."[77] Essentially this was a variation on the argument that Japan should not import economic policies that did not suit her stage of economic development. The Nagoya Chamber of Commerce pointed out the relative immaturity of Japan's economy, especially insofar as the availability of capital and the level of technology were concerned. "The economic conditions in our country . . . do not compare with those in Europe and America in such matters as the rate of interest, the scale [of enterprise], and the refinement of machinery."[78]

As the pressure for legal regulation of working conditions increased after the turn of the century, industrialists were driven to more emphatic statements of this theme. Hibiya Hizaemon, an executive of the Kanegafuchi Spinning Mills, envisaged a sharp reduction in exports leading to a massive outflow of specie and even to the exhaustion of the national treasury if the 1910 Factory Bill became law. "If it were merely a matter of health [of the workers], we would actively accept intervention. But this bill would be an extraordinary blow to Japanese industry and would obstruct our national development [*koku'un hatten*]."* Other businessmen struck a more nationalistic tone in their warnings of the adverse effects the bill would have on Japan's chance of becoming a great power, and insisted that labor must be willing to sacrifice for that goal. Tamura Masanori couched his objections in patriotic rhetoric:

Is it not true that for us to become a first-class nation by means of military power, the sweat and blood of millions of the country's people and the sacrifice of tens of thousands of lives would be required? In terms of power, this country is a second- or third-rate nation in comparison with those of Europe or America. Is it not time to call forth the earnest efforts of all the people in striving night and day to raise the country through increased productivity and the development of industry [*shokusan kōgyō*], regardless of the sacrifice?[79]

These considerations were doubtless crucial in delaying the enactment of a factory bill for nearly two decades, and forcing substantial compromises, including a fifteen-year postponement of the provision prohibiting night work, once the bill had ob-

* Quoted in Kanda, p. 7; also quoted in Kazahaya, p. 128. Another Kanegafuchi executive predicted a drop of 40 per cent in textile production if the prohibition against night work for males under 14 and women went into effect. He warned that this would mean the loss of the China market. See the interview with Fuji Masazumi in the February 25, 1910, issue of the *Tōyō Keizai Shimpō*, pp. 272–74.

tained majority support in the Diet.[80] These appeals are of interest here primarily because they illustrate the manner in which the climate of reactive nationalism served to aid Meiji businessmen in their quest for support on issues affecting private business.*

The battle over labor legislation in the Meiji period lasted more than three decades, and even so, the issue was in no sense resolved. In comparison with the history of industrial relations in the West, the most noteworthy aspect of those three decades of debate was the narrowness of the ground in dispute. There was remarkably little reference, for example, to the ideological issue of government power that had divided England only a half century before and was to dominate debates on labor laws in the United States well into the twentieth century. Specifically, there was little discussion of the sanctity of private property: no Japanese entrepreneur is recorded as having claimed the right to run his enterprise as he saw fit without outside intervention.[81] There were, it is true, some voices raised in defense of laissez-faire doctrines as they applied to labor. Mitsubishi's Shōda Hei-gorō—who, as we learned earlier, could on occasion sound very much like his American or English counterparts—proclaimed: "My own view of the labor problem is that it should be left entirely alone [jiyū ni hōnin]. The hiring and dismissal of workers should be determined by the profit to the entrepreneur and the supply and demand of labor. It is absolutely impossible to intervene or to protect by laws or other man-made means."[82] Nevertheless, Shōda ultimately fell back on the position that the adoption of Western attitudes toward labor relations would lead to "false individualism" and undermine the Japanese family system,

---

* Once again it should be said that we are not concerned here with the validity of the arguments. Whether or not Japanese industry could have competed successfully in the markets of the world if the provisions of the original factory bill had been put into effect in the 1890's (as its proponents claimed) is not relevant to the point, nor is the moral issue of "sweatshop" conditions. The point is the degree to which business spokesmen were successful in appealing to nationalistic emotions, and the effect this success had on shaping business ideology.

the root of "the beautiful customs between master and retainer" that had existed since ancient times. Because of this tradition, Shōda argued (without any apparent awareness that his argument conflicted with the laissez-faire doctrine of economic individualism), "employees loved their masters, and peace was maintained in industry through mutual dependence and mutual aid. In the absence of this emotional relationship, it would be impossible to maintain harmony in the economic world no matter how perfect the laws. As proof of this we need not look beyond the circumstances in Europe."[83]

Thus Shōda's position differed little from that of the overwhelming majority of Meiji business spokesmen, who ignored the type of ideological defense familiar in the West in order to concentrate on appeals to traditional morality and nationalist sentiment. Consequently the issues in the Meiji debate over industrial relations were limited, in the final analysis, to two questions—were the working conditions in Japanese factories sufficiently harsh to justify concern about labor agitation, and, if they were, how could this discontent be mollified without impeding industrial growth? In response to these questions, Meiji business leaders took a position consistent with the ideological position they had adopted to cope with the other problems posed by rapid industrialization: they claimed to be fulfilling the traditional role of feudal patriarchs while at the same time leading the nation's economic troops in the commercial wars with the West. Thus the identification with the samurai was taken one step further, and the new image that business spokesmen were attempting to establish was reinforced.

5. *Business Ideology and the Labor Union Movement*

The First World War and the decade that followed brought numerous changes to the Japanese business world. A new generation of executives took over the reins of Mitsui, Mitsubishi, and the other modern business enterprises. Industrialization was no longer a distant goal, but in part at least an accomplished reality; and the private sector of the economy had to a great extent outgrown its early dependence on direct government support. Moreover, the dominant position of the large *zaibatsu* concerns was now evident, and economic power was concentrated as never before in the hands of the private business elite.[1] At the same time, as the death of the Meiji oligarchs and the development of parliamentary institutions gave increased influence to the major political parties, the modern business class as a whole came to occupy a new position of importance in Japanese politics. Finally, the victory of the Allies over Germany boosted the prestige of democracy, liberalism, and individualism, and offered the prospect of a new intellectual climate in Japan.[2]

Despite these developments, Japanese business ideology underwent no substantial change. The business elite of the 1920's proved remarkably unreceptive to the wave of liberal ideas set in motion by the war. The majority of Japanese business spokesmen remained at best indifferent to the themes of economic liberalism central to the capitalist creed in the West. Economic individualism, with its emphasis on free competition, continued to occupy a very minor place in their philosophy. Individual fulfillment, personal ambition, and material incentives still received only negative mention in discussions of business activity, while patriotic devotion to national development remained the only legitimate motive of any importance for the Japanese businessman.

The Growth of the Labor Movement

So far as Japanese business leaders were concerned, labor was the dominant issue in the ideological conflicts of the 1920's. Consequently any analysis of the business creed as it was articulated in the period between the two World Wars must begin with an examination of the nature of the reaction of business to the emergence of a militant labor movement.

The attempts made to organize labor during the 1900's had by 1910 proved largely unsuccessful. In that year the government tried the anarchist leader Kōtoku Shūsui for allegedly plotting the assassination of the Emperor; and officials took advantage of the wave of indignation against radicalism to suppress left-wing activity and to drive the majority of the early union organizers underground or into exile. By 1910, there was only one labor organization of any importance left—the Yūaikai, or Friendly Society, a loosely structured association that owed its continued existence in part to the support it received from some within the business community. The Yūaikai was formed in 1912 by Suzuki Bunji, a graduate of Tokyo Imperial University who had done social welfare work for the Unitarian Church. After gaining some knowledge of the problems of the lower classes, Suzuki decided to devote himself to the problem of labor relations.[3] He sought and obtained the aid of a number of prominent businessmen, including executives of the Tokyo Electric Company, the Hirano Iron Works, and the Oe Printing Company. Soeda Jūichi, then president of the semigovernmental Kōgyō Bank (Industrial Bank), consented to serve on the Board of Advisers of the Yūaikai; and in 1915 Shibusawa Eiichi used his influence to persuade the government to allow Suzuki a passport to attend the annual convention of the American Federation of Labor.[4]

It is not surprising that businessmen looked favorably upon the Yūaikai's approach to labor problems. Suzuki, like the business spokesmen quoted in the previous chapter, argued that the problem of industrial relations in Japan differed radically from that in the West.

I believe that the Japanese worker differs from the European or American worker—at least from the American—in personality, disposition, and emotions. . . . I think that this is probably due to the great differences in national character [*kokuminsei*]. In the West everything is individualism, but in Japan we have familism. . . . Since these fundamental differences in personality appear in many and various ways, it is my feeling that differences will also manifest themselves in labor problems.[5]

In opposing the individualistic views of the West, Suzuki argued that society is a collective body [*kyōdō dantai*]. "The progress of industry depends upon cooperation and harmony between capital and labor."[6] On this basis he rejected the class-struggle doctrines of Marxist-oriented labor leaders, and told his Yūaikai members, "We cannot believe that workers can achieve well-being by overthrowing the capitalists. Unless we stand together with the capitalists, it is impossible to hope for true well-being."[7] Finally, Suzuki endorsed the paternalistic philosophy of Japanese management:

The capitalist works and creates the facilities that promote the happiness and well-being of the workers. He not only provides facilities for the education, health, and recreation of the workers, but also for death, sickness, and old age. He provides housing and encourages [the habit of] saving. In doing all this he is like a kind and loving parent and loves his children: between them there is no discord, no [problem of] obligations [*gimu*], but rather there is a spirit of mutual trust. On this basis the factory becomes exactly like a family.[8]

By 1919, however, Suzuki's hold over the Yūaikai had slipped; and the 1920's witnessed the rise of a new, more militant labor movement. The rapid industrial expansion and the inflation that had accompanied the war boom had brought hardship for wage earners. Shortly after the war the boom had given way to a sudden economic contraction, and large segments of the urban working class were put on subsistence wages or forced out of work entirely. The victory of the Western democracies and the initial success of the Russian Revolution had encouraged political agitators and radical labor leaders, who now resumed their attempts to organize a labor union movement dedicated to far-reaching social reform.[9]

The Renewed Debate over Industrial Relations

Even before the end of the war, it had become apparent that the Japanese working class was growing restive. Twice as many industrial disputes took place in 1916 as had occurred in 1915, and by 1917 this number had tripled.[10] It was partially in response to this challenge that the Japan Industrial Club (Nihon Kōgyō Kurabu) was founded in March 1917. The Club's membership included most of the prominent business figures of the day; and under the leadership of Mitsui's Dan Takuma, it became the single most important voice in industrial management in the 1920's.[11] The stated purpose of the organization was to advance industry in general by providing facilities for the exchange of ideas and for systematic research into Japan's economic problems. It was apparent from the beginning, however, that the problem of labor relations was uppermost in the minds of the Club's founders, as it was in the minds of many leaders in government and intellectual circles. At the opening ceremonies Kiyoura Keigo, the Vice-president of the Privy Council, followed former Prime Minister Okuma to the podium and declared:

I believe, as Marquis Okuma has just stated, that the problem on which the industrialists of Japan must concentrate their attention and research in the future is the problem of labor. There have already been clear manifestations of this problem in the various countries of Europe, and its beginnings have appeared in our country. . . . I believe that now that this Club has been established, if the government and the people unite, discuss things thoroughly, and achieve mutual understanding, then it certainly will be possible to proceed smoothly—even if there are a few slight disagreements.[12]

Disagreements on how best to approach the problem, however, were neither few nor slight. In a series of articles and speeches beginning in the final months of 1917, Shibusawa Eiichi added his influential voice to the increasing clamor for a new approach to industrial relations in Japan.[13] Shibusawa had come to believe that the growth of large-scale enterprises, and the changing spirit of the times, necessitated a basic change in management's attitude toward labor. While praising the traditional ethic, he argued that the philosophy of familism or *onjō shugi* was no longer adequate. Factories had grown too large for paternalism to function effectively, and workers were becoming concerned about material security. Moreover, the spread of what he termed "the mechanistic culture from the Western world" had brought with it the concept of individual rights, and in consequence workers "naturally" sought to form unions to protect their mutual interests. Thus, Shibusawa concluded in an article entitled "The Master-Retainer Morality of Old is Bankrupt," "the times change, and with the influx of Western culture it is only natural that the old master-retainer morality will be destroyed. It is absolutely impossible in today's large enterprises to maintain the close relations between the master and retainer that existed in the past, for spiritual ties are giving way to materialistic negotiations."[14] Shibusawa soon joined a number of prominent men in government in advocating the creation of a central agency, supported by funds from both government and private business, to devise and implement new means of ensuring industrial peace.[15] Early in 1919 the Home Ministry took the initiative and sought the opinions of various business organizations on the structure and function of such an agency.

The leadership of the Industrial Club was not opposed to the establishment of a central industrial agency, but it disagreed with Shibusawa's progressive views on what the agency's guiding principles should be, and how far it should go in making concessions to labor. The Executive Board responded to the Home Ministry's query with a carefully worded statement in support of the conservative ideology that had prevailed in business circles since the turn of the century. The statement expressed agreement with the view that "social problems become more complex as the organization of industry develops and the thinking of the nation undergoes change," and expressed concern that the recent war had "greatly disturbed the minds of men" and brought an influx of "foreign ideas" to the country.[16] Nevertheless, the Industrial Club considered it possible to give "proper guidance" to these new trends and thus to avoid "a hundred years of sorrow for the Imperial Nation." The solution lay not in adopting the institutions of the West, but in reemphasizing the traditional values and interpersonal relations peculiar to Japanese society.

Carefully considering the circumstances in Europe and America, we see that the spread of antagonism between capital and labor cannot be regulated through legislation. Whatever the merits of the laws, they cannot alleviate the situation. . . . Fortunately, however, there still exist today in our country the beautiful customs of antiquity. If social awareness can be urged upon the heads of business while the [level of] moral cultivation [*shūyō*] among the workers is elevated, and if both sides achieve mutual understanding and are made to realize that they share the same interests in enterprises, then there is no doubt that the labor problem can be solved on the basis of the ideals of mutual cooperation, harmony, and two-entities-in-one-body [*nisha ittai*]. In short, the evils of foreign countries can be avoided, and the merits peculiar to our country can be fostered. By these means we shall see for the first time a solution to the problem of capital and labor—*a solution unique to our country* [italics mine].[17]

It was Shibusawa's view that prevailed, however. When in November 1919 the new agency, the Kyōchōkai, issued its declaration of principles, the difference between its position and that of the Industrial Club became apparent.[18] The Kyōchōkai declaration began by coupling its appeal for harmony and compromise with an assertion of the basic equality of management and labor and the necessity that each recognize the other's rights: "*Kyōchō shugi* [the principle of harmony and conciliation] asserts that each class within society, in particular capital and labor, should respect the rights of the others on the basis of the equality of persons, while also practicing reasonable and proper self-restraint and compromise for the sake of order within society." The declaration continued with a specific attack on the shortcomings of the traditional paternalistic approach to labor management:

The consciousness of one's responsibilities is the starting point for conciliation, which must be based upon righteousness [*seigi*] and humaneness [*jindō*]. It appears today, however, that the view is steadily spreading through the world that what is known as *onjō shugi* [affectionism] is something utilized by superiors merely to placate inferiors. It must be said that *kyōchō shugi* is quite distinct from this. There is no need today to point out that differences in knowledge or circumstances do not alter the fact that people are equal. No individual can be permitted to treat another as a means. Human beings must always be ultimate ends in themselves. Respect for personality [*jinkaku*] is the root of *kyōchō shugi*.

The willingness of the Kyōchōkai to make ideological concessions to the labor movement can be seen in the rejection of *onjō shugi* and the adoption of such phrases as "just rights" (*seitō naru kenri*) and "respect for personality" (*jinkaku o sonchō*). The most important concrete concession, however, was the Kyōchōkai's proposal to grant legal recognition to labor unions: "For the sake of achieving its objectives, this association hopes . . . that labor unions and other groups will be organized, and that they will be allowed to spread and develop."[19] Japanese labor unions had been legally forbidden since the passage of the Peace Preservation Law of 1900, and although by 1919 government officials were declaring that they had no intention of using their legal power except against "radicals," labor organizations still had no legal standing.[20] Shibusawa and the Kyōchōkai were committed to the passage of a new labor law that would permit unions to function more or less as they did in Europe and America. While condemning those who would use the power of unions against the capitalist class, or encourage workers to think only of "their own selfish interests," Shibusawa argued that labor unions could provide for mutual security in the event of personal calamity, and at the same time serve, as the Yūaikai had done, to "elevate the character and personality" of the laborer.[21]

In 1920 the Hara government began serious study of the union question, and two different proposals for labor bills were drawn up. The Home Ministry submitted a draft proposing that labor unions be allowed substantial freedom to organize, enlist members, elect officers, and engage in negotiations. It even proposed freeing unions from the threat of legal liability for damages. The draft submitted by the Ministry of Agriculture and Commerce, on the other hand, placed union activities under close government supervision, restricted organization to prefectural boundaries, and limited the membership of each union to workers engaged in like occupations.[22] The disagreement between the two ministries and their supporters produced a temporary stalemate, but in 1922 the Home Ministry was given jurisdiction over labor organizations, and began drafting a labor union bill. This draft, made public in May 1925, contained most of the progressive features that had characterized the Home Ministry's proposals of 1920. By the time the bill reached the House of Representatives, however, opponents had succeeded in forcing the incorporation of many of the restrictive features originally favored by the Ministry of Agriculture and Commerce, and once again a stalemate occurred.[23] A bill drawn up by the Hamaguchi government in 1929 was passed by the House of Representatives, but was subsequently turned down by the more conservative House of Peers in February 1931.

In general, spokesmen for management groups claimed to be willing to accept moderate labor unions, but they sought a maximum of restrictions on union organization and activities. The reasons they gave for opposing a liberal labor union law reveal a remarkable continuity in Japanese business ideology insofar as labor relations are concerned. In attempting to fore-stall the establishment of labor unions, management used the same arguments it had employed against factory legislation in the 1900's: 1) Japan's unique cultural heritage made Western institutions undesirable; and 2) the necessity of competing with the West made greater concessions to labor impossible. Let us see how these arguments were developed by business spokes-men in the 1920's and early 1930's.

The Defense of Japan's Cultural Heritage

It was the first of these themes—the conflict between Japanese tradition and Western ideas—that received the greatest em-phasis in the debate over labor unions. Despite mounting criti-cism, few Japanese businessmen were prepared to abandon the philosophy of familism. The rationale of this approach to indus-trial relations was based on the claim that Japanese society dif-fered in essence from Western societies. In 1919 Fujiyama Raita, who headed the Association of Japanese Chambers of Com-merce, insisted that labor problems could not be solved unless this difference was recognized, and he reminded his readers of the special nature of the Japanese national polity (*kokutai*) with its "unbroken line of Emperors." To Fujiyama, the tradi-tional solidarity of the Japanese family was one of the main rea-sons for the difference between Japan and the rest of the world, and he argued that this solidarity was so closely related to the philosophy of paternalism in industrial relations that one could not be altered without the other being affected. He predicted dire social consequences if foreign ideas such as individualism and legal rights were allowed to subvert the values associated with the Japanese family ethic: "Even among parents and children there is a tendency [these days] to advocate rights; parents neglect their children, and children refuse to help their parents even when the parents are poverty-stricken. [It is as if] they were horses and oxen or not related to one another at all."[24] Another business executive writing in the same magazine also emphasized the difference between the Japanese national polity (*kokutai*) and the social order in other countries, which he argued resulted from the fact that in other countries the people were of mixed racial origins, while in Japan "those above and those below are all one race [*minzoku*], one family."[25]

As Japanese businessmen became subject to more and more pressure from abroad to make Japanese labor practices conform to international standards, the theme of Japan's cultural uniqueness began to dominate discussions of paternalism. When the subject of an international labor agency was discussed at the Paris Peace Conference, the Industrial Club sent the Japanese delegation this cable:

In the present situation of the working class of our country, there are differences in national customs, in the habits of the people, and in social circumstances; the situation of the workers is not the same as that in Western countries. Consequently it is difficult to import and adopt directly the institutions and laws of foreign countries. Moreover, we believe that it would not necessarily be in the best interests of the nation to aim at making labor conditions uniform with those in other countries.[26]

Mutō Sanji, who served as chief representative of Japanese management at the 1919 Washington Conference on labor, expressed the same views: "I find most of the current arguments put forward regarding [the labor problem] utterly unconvincing, because they are either representing some special standpoints or [are] mere translations of the Western arguments. . . . I must emphasize in this connection the fact that nothing would be more mistaken than to simply copy the Western systems."[27] Like Fujiyama, Mutō expressed fear that the spread of the concept of legal rights would dissolve traditional ties of sentiment and poison relations between Japanese management and labor. To counteract "senseless attacks on the principle of familial affection [*kazokuteki onjō shugi*]" and to prevent Japanese laborers from becoming "as radical as those in Europe," Mutō proposed the formation of a nationwide association of Japanese employers, dedicated to teaching the public the true meaning of paternalism.[28]

The claim that the demand for legal rights for labor unions was inspired by foreign models unsuited to Japan continued to figure prominently in the campaigns against new labor legislation. In 1925 the Industrial Club responded to government proposals with demands for numerous amendments that would have placed severe limitations on union activities. The Club justified its position thus:

We have heard the explanation put forward that this draft of a labor union bill was drawn up on the basis of the Versailles Treaty, that to alter this bill would be to violate that treaty, and that since our country ratified the treaty, we must by all means respect it. . . . [But the treaty states], "Each industrial nation should endeavor to apply the provisions concerning labor insofar as the special circumstances of that country permit." In accordance with this, we believe that it would be best to pass a law appropriate to our own national circumstances.[29]

The proposals of the Hamaguchi government in 1929 met with the objection that a liberal labor union law would "lead to the destruction of the capitalist-labor relationship peculiar to our country." The Industrial Club insisted on provisions to protect those workers who did not wish to join unions: "The great majority of workers do not belong to labor unions, [because] they are part of the employment relationship peculiar to our country, which is based on mutual sentiment between capital and labor—[a relationship] that can be considered an extension of the family system."

In arguing against the adoption of "foreign" approaches to the problems of industrial relations, Japanese business spokesmen were asserting that such approaches were both undesirable and unnecessary. It was argued that the workers in Western countries had no choice but to make demands on the basis of individual rights, while Japanese workers could rely on a tradition of paternal benevolence. As Mutō Sanji said:

There have been [*sic*] arisen of late among scholars and publicists strong objections to paternalism in the relations between capital and labour. . . . I think that those who are opposed to paternalism hold the view that it is to the interests of labour to settle labour problems by question of right [sic]. Such views come only from the fallacy of disregarding differences in conditions between Western and Japanese labouring men. No record of paternalism is to be found in the history of Western countries. So it is quite natural that Western labourers should always claim their rights.[30]

In the same vein, the Association of Industrial Organizations of the Kantō Region argued that there was no need for the government to create legal minimums for working conditions: "Our industrial world is controlled by the spirit of familism, and by our national character, which prizes moral obligations [*giri*] and humaneness [*ninjō*] more highly than legal obligations [*gimu*] or rights [*kenri*]. . . . The many welfare provisions that have been developed within our country's enterprises are truly the direct manifestation of this spirit, for they have all been the result of independent action on the part of the owners of these enterprises, rather than the result of laws."[31]

This position—that neither the help of labor organizations nor the intervention of the government was necessary to promote the interests of the workers—was of course vulnerable to demands that management demonstrate its sincerity by granting the reductions in working hours, the increased wages, and the expanded welfare facilities that union leaders requested. Management's answer to this formed the second half of the argument advanced against the labor movement of the 1920's and early 1930's—the claim that Japanese industry could not afford greater concessions to labor. In 1925 and 1929, for instance, the Industrial Club prefaced its objections to proposed labor laws with a warning against placing further obstacles in the path of industrial development. "The industry of our country is still in the first stages of development," the 1925 statement began. "We are deficient in natural resources and are forced to rely on other countries for raw materials for manufacturing." The lack of natural resources, the limited amount of arable land, and "the increase in population of almost a million each year," the Industrial Club leaders asserted in 1929, had already placed a heavy burden on the Japanese economy. As a consequence, Japan was at a serious disadvantage in the competition for world markets. "Our country occupies one corner of Asia and must compete with neighbors like Russia and China, who are rich in raw materials and cheap labor. We also feel keenly the commercial and industrial threat of America across the Pacific. Given these facts, anyone can understand the difficulties involved in attempting to stimulate exports and restrict imports." Japan's precarious economic position, therefore, required "tremendous effort and hard work." Business leaders insisted that this, rather than a lack of paternalistic concern, was the real reason they resisted union demands for better working conditions or higher wages.[32]

Spokesmen for Japanese management were not content, however, to appeal to tradition and the need to compete with foreign industrial powers. They attacked the motives of labor leaders, charging that the real aim of the labor movement was to undermine the Japanese economy and foment revolution. Labor unions, they pointed out, had emerged "under the influence of socialism," which was "rampant" in Europe. "These radicals [i.e., unionists] of course call themselves moderates, [but] they are not concerned with the promotion of industry on the basis of harmony and concord."[33] According to a "statement of purpose" issued by the National Federation of Industrial Organizations (Zenkoku Sangyō Dantai Rengōkai), an employer association formed in 1931 for the specific purpose of fighting labor unions, it would be disastrous to make concessions: "The danger steadily grows greater that the radical labor and social movements will destroy industry and block national progress."[34] It was on these grounds that business justified their demands for tight restrictions on the qualifications for union membership and for holding union office. "Foreigners have come [to Japan] to turn unions toward radicalism," they alleged;[35] and unless the government maintained careful control, the true interests of the workers would be "sacrificed to the ambitions of a small number of agitators."[36]

Thus, in the 1920's business reaction to the labor movement was substantially what it had been during the campaign for factory legislation in the Meiji period; the appeal to traditional norms and the claim that these norms set Japan apart from all other societies had not altered. We must now turn to the question of why businessmen believed that no new approach to labor relations was necessary; why they rejected the assertion of Shibusawa and others that paternalism was unsuited to the times.

The Success of the Appeal to Tradition

In the 1920's as in the 1900's, Japanese business leaders found themselves in a position where acceptance of the Western approach to industrial relations would have entailed certain substantial concessions to labor. These management was not prepared to grant. Although it is not our concern here to determine whether or not Japanese industry could in reality have afforded such concessions, it is important to note that the 1920's were a decade of retrenchment and economic insecurity for Japanese business, particularly for the modern sector of private industry, which was the one most affected by the trends in international trade. More relevant, however, are the reasons why management became convinced that it need not make concessions or alter its ideological position.

Labor union leaders had little success in their attempt to organize Japanese workers in the 1920's. Despite the considerable progress made in industrialization, the composition of the labor force and the character of the industrial workplace had changed little since the Meiji period. As late as 1928, over 42 per cent of the industrial workers in Japan still labored in factories employing a hundred workers or less.[37] The percentage of women in factories also remained high—over 50 per cent—throughout the 1920's.[38] The intimacy of the small factory and the difficulty of organizing women workers thus remained important obstacles to the development of a broad-based labor movement despite the increasing numerical strength of the laboring class. Union

leaders too suffered frustration in their efforts to organize workers, even in those enterprises where the size of the factories and
the proportion of adult males were larger. The promise of lifelong employment, previously limited largely to the white-collar
workers (*shokuin*), was increasingly extended to production
workers (*kōin*) after the First World War. With this came a
wage structure based primarily upon length of service (*nenkō
joretsu*), and an elaborate system of family allowances, welfare
provisions, and other fringe benefits.[39] Although the adoption of
these policies represented significant changes in the sphere of
actual practice, they did not entail any susbstantial changes in
business ideology. On the contrary, management was simply ap-
plying the principles it claimed to have been following from the
early Meiji period.*

Another factor—education—can also be said to have reinforced conservative attitudes among Japanese workers and
thereby to have hindered the efforts of union leaders who sought
to make use of slogans and ideas imported from the West. The
village environment became less of a factor in influencing the
attitudes of workers as the labor force came to include more and
more individuals raised in the city. But primary education had
become almost universal by the end of the Meiji period, and as a
result, by 1924 some 80 per cent of all Japanese factory workers
had been exposed to six years of formal schooling in which great
emphasis was placed on respect for hierarchy, loyalty to the
State, and the duty of laboring diligently in order to fulfill one's
obligation to society.[40] It is therefore not surprising that employers expected even workers from urban environments to re-

* Japanese scholars have emphasized the changes in labor practices and
characterized them as part of a transition from the traditional "master-
retainer paternalism" (*shujū kankei no onjō shugi*) of the Tokugawa
period to a new "familial paternalism" (*kazoku kankei no onjō shugi*).
As we have seen, however, business leaders in the Meiji period were already speaking of the traditional relationship between employer and employee in terms of family-like ties. Thus Professor Hazama Hiroshi, in his
study of personnel administration, has noted how difficult it is to define
the difference between these two concepts insofar as the ideology of paternalism in Japanese business is concerned; see his *Nihon rōmu kanrishi*,
pp. 43–47.

spond to appeals to these values. This of course gave business-men a considerable tactical advantage, insofar as they represented themselves as defenders of orthodox social doctrines, fighting against the "foreign radicalism" of Marxist socialism and "Western materialism." While the spokesmen for American capitalism fought labor legislation and union organization on the grounds that they were collectivistic and therefore inimical to the traditional American values of individual freedom and responsibility,[41] Japanese businessmen tended naturally to stress the incompatibility of foreign concepts of individual rights and contractual relations with the collectivistic values of Japanese tradition. Ultimately, as we shall see, this collectivistic orientation made the justification of private profit more difficult and thus rendered the business elite highly vulnerable to the type of attack launched by right-wing critics during the next twenty years. In the 1920's, however, the response of management to the threat posed by left-wing labor unions proved quite successful. Union membership remained less than 300,000 until 1928—and even that figure greatly magnifies the actual gains made by the union movement, since it includes small groups and company unions that took little part in the main movement.[42] The demands for a fairer share for labor, and threats of class warfare to obtain it, had forced Japanese management to defend its paternalistic approach; but when labor leaders proved unable to mobilize Japanese workers behind these demands, the case for a new approach to labor relations was lost.

Success in another sphere also influenced business attitudes toward the wave of liberal and egalitarian ideas that emanated from the West. By the 1920's the business elite in Japan had already gained a measure of political power.[43] True, their position proved to be a highly precarious one, dependent as it was on the power of the political parties in the Diet, and its importance should not be exaggerated. Yet in contrast to the situation in mid-nineteenth–century England, where the business class had found the support of the working classes and the slogans of liberalism of great value in their struggle against the entrenched aristocracy, in twentieth-century Japan there was good reason for businessmen to believe that their political enemies stood to gain more than they themselves did from any significant change in the distribution of political power.[44] Businessmen were therefore understandably wary of social doctrines that might be used to sanction the extension of suffrage and other rights to the working classes. The manner in which business spokesmen attempted to defend capitalism as an economic system reflected this wariness.

6. *The Japanese Business Elite and the Defense of Capitalism*

The problem of defending capitalism as an economic system did not loom large in the public statements of Meiji business leaders. This was partly because of the difficulty they found in discussing profit incentives while denying an interest in material rewards, and in extolling private competition while seeking government aid and urging harmony on labor. More importantly, the immediate issues involving business interests in the Meiji period seem not to have been thought of by businessmen as a challenge to the system of private enterprise. Although the theory of socialism enjoyed a great vogue among the Meiji intellectuals, and many leaders of the nascent labor movement of the 1900's spoke in terms of "class struggle" and "the inevitable decline of capitalism," the major threat to business interests in the Meiji period came from the more moderate reformers and their allies within the government bureaucracy. The views of these groups owed less to the slogans of the early socialists than they did to the doctrines propagated by leading members of the Association for the Study of Social Policy (Shakai Seisaku Gakkai).

Capitalism and the Social Policy School

The Association for the Study of Social Policy had been organized in 1898 as a forum in which to debate important social and economic issues. Although the proceedings of the annual conferences reveal a variety of basic views, it is clear that many of the Association's most active members were influenced by the arguments for social reform set forth by Ludwig (Lujo) Brentano, Adolf Wagner, and the other German economists who made up the group known as the *Kathedersozialisten*.[1] Among those influenced was Kanai Noboru, a German-educated professor of economics at the University of Tokyo, who believed that Japan could escape radical socialism only by adopting a comprehensive system of social legislation on the model of that found in Bismarckian Germany.[2] Kanai and others of his persuasion at the University of Tokyo had considerable influence among members of the government bureaucracy (many of whom were graduates of that university), and it was they who spearheaded the campaign for factory legislation in the Meiji period, arguing that legal controls on private enterprise were necessary to ensure harmony between the social classes.[3] Their influence may be seen in the Association's prospectus, which states that the Association was opposed to the principle of laissez-faire because "the rise of extreme self-interest and unrestrained free competition" could lead to a "great disparity in wealth" and result in social conflict.[4] Despite these dangers, however, Kanai and the other authors of the prospectus were convinced that private capitalism was the only practical means of realizing economic progress. Thus Kanai and a number of noted political economists, including Fukuda Tokuzō, Wada Gakikenzō, and Kuwada Kumazō, engaged the Japanese socialists in a running debate over the relative merits of socialism and private enterprise. In their defense of capitalism they employed many of the arguments familiar in the West. For example, a statement issued in 1901 proclaimed: "The foundations of the present economic system are twofold—free competition and private property.... These two are prime requisites for economic progress. Those who would abolish them ... would return us to a prehistoric age.[5] In his rejection of socialism, Kuwada Kumazō claimed that the possibility of amassing private property served as an incentive to effort, and argued further that the private enterprise system was the most efficient means of determining the division of labor within society.[6]

The arguments propagated by these members of the Association for the Study of Social Policy formed the theoretical basis for the defense of capitalism in Japan during the years from 1900 to 1930.[7] The intellectuals who staffed the Kyōchōkai, the agency created with government aid in 1919 to seek solutions to labor problems, announced that the new organization subscribed to the principles of the German school of *Sozialpolitik*, and that like the Association for the Study of Social Policy, the Kyōchōkai was dedicated to pointing a middle way between the extremes of economic individualism and radical socialism.[8] Like the economists quoted above, the spokesmen for the Kyōchōkai defended capitalism primarily in terms of the end results, admitting that it was a far from perfect system: "Capitalism ... has many defects, but it has one great virtue. It is the most effective system of increasing the production of wealth and materials at reduced prices."[9] In their eyes, capitalism's biggest drawback was that it created an imbalance in the distribution of wealth by limiting the individual worker's lack of bargaining power. On these grounds the Kyōchōkai urged the immediate enactment of progressive social legislation that would permit labor to organize, and would ensure a more just distribution of the fruits of capitalism.

Justice did not entail absolute equality, as Tazawa Yoshiharu, Managing Director of the Kyōchōkai, explained; rewards should vary with the contribution of individuals: "Basically, there is no absolute equality among men in physique, character, or intelligence. Consequently there can be no equality in the value of their spiritual contribution to human culture nor in the spiritual compensation they realize from it. By the same token, there can never be equality in the capacity for production that they contribute to economic activity nor in the distribution that arises from it." The reference to "spiritual compensation" is important. In contrast to the theorists of the early Social Policy school, who stressed the necessity of material rewards as incentives to individual effort, the Kyōchōkai writers tended to avoid the concept of material incentives in favor of an ethic of work performance in which work became all but an end in itself, quite apart from any material reward that might be realized: "We advocate, as a basic moral concept, *kinrō shugi*—the will to work. Without work, social progress and the advancement of mankind cannot be expected. We firmly believe that human life is the pursuit of an eternal ideal, and that the pursuit of this ideal can only be undertaken through labor and effort. In this sense, work is a virtue in itself." Tazawa explicitly rejected any materialistic interpretation of the end purpose of work: "There are, however, erroneous views of work. One such view holds that it is merely a means of earning a living. Another interprets it as a means of obtaining pleasure. . . . [The popular view] takes as the highest human goal the satisfaction of material desires, and considers that the possession of wealth is the means of achieving this. Work is recognized only as a means to wealth. . . . Our view of work is entirely different." On these grounds the Kyōchōkai condemned both the idle rich and those laborers who succumbed to "selfishness" in their demands for unreasonably short hours or high wages.[10]

Although the Kyōchōkai's proposals for more progressive labor legislation were rejected by most business leaders, the ideal of achieving "conciliation and harmony between individualism and collectivism" had great appeal for the Japanese business class in the 1920's and 1930's.[11] In the attempt to project an image that would serve to allay the growing hostility toward capitalism, Japanese business spokesmen utilized many of the same arguments developed by the Kyōchōkai writers.

The Self-Image of the Managerial Elite

The ideology of the managerial elite of the 1920's and 1930's was substantially the same as that of the Meiji entrepreneur. Although the symbol of the warrior armed with an abacus was less and less used as death depleted the ranks of businessmen

who could claim to have once served as samurai,* the appeal
for authority was still based on the assertion that the business
elite were dedicated to utilizing their talents for the welfare
of the nation rather than for private ends. The main focus had,
however, shifted slightly to reflect their new concern with the
problems of labor relations. Even greater emphasis was now
placed on the organic nature of industrial society and the interdependence of management and labor. Pamphlets distributed
among the workers stressed the importance of cooperation and
one quoted an edict in which the Emperor had charged his subjects to "bear in mind the ideal of *kyōson kyōei* (living and pros-
pering together)."[12] A Mitsui executive explained that *kyōson
kyōei* was Mitsui's guiding principle: "The literal translation of
'*kyōson*' is 'mutual existence.' . . . And this mutual existence, you
must understand, is the fundamental principle of the House of
Mitsui in its relations with its associates and employees and
even with what you call the consumer, the buying public. . . .
You cannot exist alone. You have to exist with others. What is
good for one must be believed good for others."[13] For all to prosper there must be leadership, said business spokesmen. Mutō
Sanji explained that leadership was the function of the capitalist
class: "If [the workers] remember the fact that no business can
be undertaken without someone leading it, they must resign
themselves to the circumstances in which they are led by capitalists." Even if the workers should set up their own enterprises,
Mutō continued, it was abundantly clear that in the course of
time leaders would arise among them to direct the businesses.
"In other words, businesses will eventually be led by capitalists."[14]

Some executives preferred to disavow the label "capitalist"

---

* The samurai origins of *early* business leaders continued to receive
prominent mention in the biographies published during the 1920's and
1930's: see, *e.g.*, Hara, III, 6ff; and Shirayanagi, pp. 192–96. Moreover,
some of the new generation of business leaders, although born too late to
have served as samurai under the Tokugawa regime, could proudly lay
claim to having been raised in ex-samurai families; see the interview with
Ikeda Seihin (1867–1950) in Hōchi Shimbunsha Keizaibu, pp. 63–67.

altogether. Dan Takuma answered the accusation that the capitalist class oppressed the workers by claiming, "The managers of the enterprises are, in reality, one type of worker."[15] Referring to the fact that most leading Japanese businessmen were salaried executives rather than owners, Dan argued that the existence in Japan of a separate managerial class had served to check any tendencies toward oppression on the part of capitalist-owners. "The men of enterprise control the capitalists. . . . In truth, nowhere in the world are the capitalists as weak as they are in Japan."* Tsuda Shingo, Mutō's successor as head of the Kanegafuchi Spinning Mills, insisted, "I am not a capitalist. I am an employee of the company and a servant of society."[16]

Occasionally, as in the statement by Mutō Sanji quoted above, it was suggested that members of the working class could aspire to rise to the ranks of leadership. Kuhara Fusanosuke, founder of one of the "new" *zaibatsu* and a prominent political figure in the 1930's, remarked on this possibility: "It should not be forgotten that workers are not necessarily fated to remain workers forever. If they do their work properly, they will gradually become capitalists."[17] The opportunity for upward mobility was not, however, a central theme as it had been in the classic Anglo-American business ideology, where the claim that opportunities existed for all was invoked as proof that success was a product of individual ability and therefore ought to be appropriately rewarded.[18] In Japanese business ideology, by contrast, such statements appear as isolated remarks incidental to the main themes of cooperation, devotion to duty, and the eschewal of private interests. The qualities making for success are discussed far less in terms of individual merit or the attributes that distinguish leaders than in terms of the fulfillment of one's assigned function: that is to say, success is defined

---

* Ko Dan Danshaku Denki Hensan Iinkai, II, 43. Dan's biographers elaborated: "[Dan's]views regarding labor unions stemmed from his own experience as a manager whose position between capital and labor made it possible for him to understand the psychology of the workers. Therefore, his view differed from the so-called 'capitalist spirit' based on individualism."

in terms of the determination to work conscientiously and diligently whatever one's position rather than in terms of superior abilities. Of all the qualities ascribed to successful businessmen in the 1920's and 1930's, the willingness to work was by far the most important. As Baba Eiichi, the president of the Kangyō Bank, put it: "I believe in effort (*dōryoku*). The cardinal rule for those young men who would succeed should be to exert themselves without complaint in whatever position they are placed."*

Managerial leadership in the 1920's and 1930's, as well as during most of the Meiji period, was pictured primarily in terms of ability to enlist cooperation and bring about harmony. In 1928 Fujiwara Ginjiro, the chief executive of the Oji Paper Company, had this to say of the former Mitsui leader Asabuki Eiji: "The one feature of Asabuki's outstanding personality that I admired most was his deep conciliatory character (*chōwasei*). Asabuki was involved in many knotty problems in the political as well as business world; but since he was able to understand both sides [of a dispute], once he stepped into a problem he would bring about a smooth solution to the matter."[19] The ability to handle men and avoid discord was the characteristic most highly praised in discussions of talented business executives. In American business ideology the typical entrepreneur has been most often portrayed as a man of great imagination and courage who, seeing what other men are unable to see, rebels against social convention to achieve some innovating breakthrough. These qualities received only secondary mention, if they were mentioned at all, for Japanese business ideology stressed what has been termed the "cooperative" rather than

* In speaking of themselves, Japanese business executives were fond of stressing how hard they worked. For example, in 1928 the newspaper *Hōchi Shimbun* ran a long series of brief, informal interviews with over a hundred and fifty of Japan's most prominent businessmen. One of the questions asked concerned hobbies, and out of the variety of responses, the most common was that the executive being questioned had no time for interests outside his work—that work took up all his time and energies. See Hōchi Shimbunsha Keizaibu, pp. 9, 38–41, 52, 79–82, 100, 112–15, 133–34, 154, 156, 196–99, 211–14, and 318.

the "creative" component of entrepreneurship. In Albert O. Hirschman's phrase, the important thing was to possess "the ability to engineer agreement among all interested parties ... the ability to bring together and hold together an able staff, to delegate authority, to inspire loyalty, to handle successfully relations with labor and the public, and a host of other managerial talents."[20] It was these "managerial" talents, difficult as they were to define precisely, that were most often praised in Japanese business ideology. Usually the implication was that these were innate abilities. Prominent mention was often made of an executive's educational background, but emphasis was placed on the prestige thus acquired rather than on any technical expertise or special knowledge that might have been acquired through formal schooling. Discussions of success by Japanese businessmen were almost always accompanied by admonitions against selfish ambition and striving for material rewards. While acting as president of the Industrial Club and head of the Mitsui enterprises, Dan Takuma wrote numerous articles and speeches on the meaning of success in business. For example, in 1924, Dan advised a large assembly of young men who were planning careers in commerce or industry, "If you are in an enterprise, no matter what it is that you do, that is your own Heaven-given function [*tenshoku*]. If you are successful in this and make some contribution to the Nation and your fellow countrymen, the sense of having contributed is your compensation. If you are fortunate, fame and wealth will perhaps be granted you, but these compensations should come as natural by-products. They are not the ultimate aim."[21] Writing in the *Jitsugyō no Nihon* a few years later, Dan elaborated:

People who believe that happiness can be gained by piling up large sums of money must be said to be greatly mistaken. ... For true happiness, the heart must be content; there must be spiritual security. Happiness on the spiritual plane lies in rendering service to others and to society. ... The men who have attained spiritual happiness, who can be described as contented in their hearts, are those who are spurred on by the pious ideal of selflessness [*muga*]; who put their hearts and strength into the work entrusted to them without

thought of compensation or calculation of profit or loss; who think of
fulfilling their tasks one by one; and who work with all their might,
using their best efforts.[22]

Like the Kyōchōkai, Japanese business spokesmen emphasized an ethic of work performance all but divorced from considerations of material incentives and reward. The willingness
of the Japanese businessman to work for "spiritual" compensation—for the satisfaction of contributing to society—was frequently contrasted with the "utilitarian" (*korishugi*), "individualistic" (*kojin shugi*), and "selfish" (*riko shugi*) views attributed to businessmen in Western societies. Zen Keinosuke, an
insurance executive and pamphleteer for the National Federation of Industrial Organizations, described the difference thus:

The attitude of Japanese businessmen toward business is not the
self-centered, individualistic attitude of the Americans or Europeans.
Once a [Japanese] has been given responsibility for a business, even
if someone should say "Over here there are more profitable conditions
and you can make more money," he will reply, "No, this is my business. I must make a success of this business."
    Once he has undertaken [a job] he desires to make that business,
that company, a thing of beauty. His business and his life are one.
This attitude corresponds to something distinct from the calculation
of profit and loss. This is the true attitude—this is the spirit of management in Japanese industry.[23]

In eulogizing Dan Takuma, the president of the National Federation of Industrial Organizations spoke of Dan's refusal to
succumb to American ways of thinking about business enterprise:

He went abroad to study in Boston, the cultural center of America,
and absorbed to the fullest the cultural, spiritual and technical learning there. . . . But although he received his education in America and
breathed the atmosphere of liberalism, his own spirit remained completely that of a Japanese samurai. He did not follow the theories of
America or Europe with regard to economic and social questions;
rather, he based his thinking on the national circumstances of Japan;
on the Japanese national character; and he considered morality to

be the essence of industrial management. He loved his business as he did his children, and he devoted his life to it. Profit-making was of secondary importance to him.[24]

Makino Motojirō, president of the Fudōchōkin Bank and author of several works on proper business attitudes, made the same point in more trenchant language: "Those who will do nothing except for profit do not have the true spirit of a Japanese. They have the head of a foreigner. They are detestable."[25]

In articulating this view of work and success, Japanese business leaders were consciously attempting to modify the attitudes that seemed to be at the root of the widespread hostility toward the business class. Hirao Hachisaburō, who was later to become the national president of the Greater Japan Patriotic Industrial Association (Dai Nippon Sangyō Hōkoku Kai), contrasted the widespread animosity toward the capitalist class in Japan that existed in the 1920's with the praise given to capitalists by intellectuals and journalists in America. He concluded that it was the lack of social consciousness evinced by capitalists such as the family heads of Mitsui, Sumitomo, and Mitsubishi, who neither took an active part in running their enterprises nor devoted themselves to public or charitable affairs, that alienated the public. He therefore urged them to fulfill their obligations by working actively and directly for the good of society.[26] In the eulogy of Dan Takuma cited above, Gō Seinosuke noted that it is easy for men to succumb to self-interest in commercial pursuits—"This is the reason for the tendency to be contemptuous of businessmen and insult them"—and he praised Dan's effort to "raise the quality of businessmen."[27] Mutō Sanji wrote of the need for a national association of employers that would "use every opportunity to make it known to the public that ... employers are always primarily concerned with the public good."[28]

The remarkable aspect of the attempt by business leaders in the 1920's to allay hostility toward the business class is the absence of arguments aimed at justifying private enterprise as an economic institution. Business spokesmen were quite articulate in defending the motives and characters of private businessmen, but it was not until the 1930's that they felt called upon to defend capitalism as a system.

The 1930's and the Attack from the Right

In the 1930's a new threat to Japanese capitalism emerged in the form of a vigorous and often fanatical right-wing political movement. A complex amalgam of militarism, agrarianism, fascism, and "ultranationalism" or "Japanism," the movement owed its unity partly to a common animosity toward the *zaibatsu* and the existing political parties, which were accused of conspiring to oppress the people and subvert traditional Japanese morality. The views of one right-wing group were summarized at a trial of a number of its members who were accused of plotting the overthrowal of the government in 1931: "The political parties, the *zaibatsu*, and a small privileged group attached to the ruling class are all sunk in corruption. They conspire in parties to pursue their egoistic interests and desires, to the neglect of national defense and to the confusion of government."[29]

1931 marked the emergence of the radical right as a dangerous threat. The depression had grown steadily worse after 1927, and the 1930 Naval Disarmament Conference in London had created new resentments. Subsequently two plots against parliamentary government were uncovered in March and October of 1931. The upsurge of chauvinist feeling accompanying the Manchurian Incident in September gave businessmen more cause for serious concern about anti-capitalist sentiment among the ultranationalists and the military. The Mitsui Company posted bodyguards to protect its key executives,[30] but despite such precautions, Mitsui's chief director Dan Takuma was among those killed in the spring of 1932 by right-wing extremists seeking to bring about a new political and economic order by assassinating prominent business and political figures. 1933 and 1934 brought revelations of new plots; and in February 1936 the terrorist tactics of the radical right culminated in an armed mutiny and an attempted coup led by officers of the Army and Navy.[31]

The fear of armed rebellion and mass assassination subsided after the February 1936 incident, but with the outbreak of war with China in 1937 came the final collapse of parliamentary government in Japan. Political power had shifted to the upper echelons of the civil and military bureaucracies, and the demands of the new leaders for general mobilization posed the threat of increased governmental control over the economy through the nationalization of key industries. Army spokesmen proclaimed:

It is of paramount importance to adapt all national activities to war conditions; to place manpower, material, and all other visible and invisible resources at the disposal of the government. . . . The scope of general mobilization is far-reaching. It includes guidance of national morale in time of war, supplementation of insufficient resources, realignment of financial organs, control and allocation of war materials, and other appertaining [sic] measures.[32]

Thus in the 1930's Japanese business leaders found themselves faced with a foe over whom they no longer held an advantage, as they had with their liberal and Marxist opponents in preceding decades. Whereas in the 1920's businessmen had been able to say they were defending traditional Japanese social doctrines against the "foreign radicalism" of socialism and labor unionism, now the tables were turned, and it was the right wing that had assumed the role of champion of the traditional virtues. As a consequence, the business elite was put on the defensive and was forced to attempt to justify the institution of private property, the competitive pursuit of profit, and the importance of private initiative.

The Defense of Private Capitalism

Individual businessmen differed in their enthusiasm for military expansion, especially as increased involvement on the Asian continent led to the possibility of a full-scale war against the United States;* but business leaders were not slow to recognize the threat to their common interests posed by right-wing attacks on private capitalism. Speaking of the assassination of Dan Takuma in 1932, Yano Tsuneta called the murder a blow aimed at the business community as a whole, and described it as part of a plot to "reform Japan by eliminating the capitalists." Attributing such hostility to the persistence of "feudalistic" thinking about economics, Yano urged his colleagues to emphasize the contribution that capitalism had made to the advancement of civilization in general and the development of Japan in particular:

Japan has become one of the great powers in the world. Who is responsible for this? I believe that if the pre-capitalist economic system had been preserved, not a trace of Japan would be left today. Some say it is because of education or the military that Japan has come so far, but I say that if the economy had failed, then there would have been no development in education among the military.... It is capitalism, given free rein in the world, that has brought about this economic development.[33]

The argument that capitalism had proven itself the most effective means to economic progress was coupled with the assertion that government bureaucracies were inherently incapable of operating business enterprises. Matsunaga Yasuzaemon, a director of several large electric power companies, who retired rather than accept the nationalization of his industry, was vehement in his denunciation of government control. He created

---

* It is common to distinguish between the "new *zaibatsu*" leaders, such as Kuhara Fusanosuke and Ayukawa Gisuke, whose business interests were closely connected with the armaments industries and the exploitation of Manchuria, and the executives of Mitsui and the older established firms, who had equally important interests in a peacetime economy. But the questions of how these vested interests affected business views of military expansion and what role, if any, business leaders played in the decisions that led to war have yet to receive adequate treatment by political historians. Perhaps the most plausible generalization is offered by Edwin O. Reischauer who believes that "the average *zaibatsu* executive remained afraid of the risks and expense of a major war, but he was not adverse to cooperating with the militarists in minor colonial ventures and in the profits of building an empire." Reischauer, pp. 179–80.

something of a sensation in the press in 1938 by telling an audience that included a number of government officials: "The promotion of industry cannot be left to the efforts and independent will of you [bureaucrats]. To entrust it to the bureaucracy would be outrageous. Bureaucrats are the dregs of humanity, and so long as this decision [to nationalize the power industry] goes unchanged, there can be no hope for the development of Japan."[34] Kuhara Fusanosuke, himself active in right-wing political circles, argued: "In order to promote efficiency, you must have competition. There is no competition when bureaucrats [manage business]; therefore [business] would naturally be inefficient."[35] Despite capitalism's defects, Kuhara insisted, it was superior to government management, which he equated with Communism: "The planned economy of the bureaucratic system is a manifestation of Communism.... Because the government monopolizes all aspects of industry, neither private industry nor private property is permitted. Since the people are not free, and the government manages all of industry, efficiency obviously cannot develop and defeat in international competition is unavoidable."[36] The necessity of economic freedom for economic progress was also stressed by Tsuda Shingo, head of the Kanegafuchi Spinning Mills: "Industry must be free. Japanese industry is but newly born and must now grow. Therefore it would be terrible if we were to imitate the old countries of Europe and impose controls. Industry must be entirely free. Only if it is free can Japan, which is still young, grow."[37]

Business spokesmen also rallied to the defense of private ownership. In 1936 the president of the Electric Power Association (Denki Kyōkai) denounced the Hirota government's proposal to nationalize the generation of electric power, calling it "a violation of the article in the Constitution protecting private property."* When the Electric Power Control Bill finally

* Ikeo Yoshizō, article in the August 1, 1936, issue of the magazine *Ekonomisuto* (The Economist), p. 20. The reference is to Article XXVII of the Constitution, which states: "the right of property of every Japanese

reached the floor of the Diet in 1938, the Japan Economic Federation (Nihon Keizai Renmeikai) petitioned the government to withdraw the bill, saying, "This bill would attempt to create state control of electric power, which is contrary to the concept of property rights that have heretofore existed in our country. This would cause the creative initiative of the people in our enterprises to wither and decline."[38]

The vagueness of the reference to private property as a necessary incentive to "creative initiative" is typical of the manner in which business spokesmen even in the mid-1930's avoided explicit discussion of the profit motive. In 1940, however, representatives of seven of the most influential business organizations in Japan issued a joint resolution setting forth their opposition to any further extension of government controls.[39] The resolution included a section demanding "recognition of the concept of profit, to the extent to which it is in accord with national objectives." The authors of the resolution stated:

It is wrong to repudiate the pursuit of profit, to overemphasize *messhi hōkō* [the principle of extinction of self in service to the nation], or to spread the erroneous idea that private profit conflicts with national objectives. . . . At present the pursuit of profit is being denounced in our country, despite the fact that it not only does not hinder but actually stimulates such things as exports, which are the source of funds for needed imports. . . . We advocate that the profit

---

subject shall remain inviolable. Measures necessary to be taken for the public benefit shall be provided for by law." This legal doctrine was reaffirmed in 1925 when the Diet enacted the Peace Preservation Law specifically forbidding political activity aimed at "altering the system of private ownership of property." Business spokesmen, however, found it difficult to base their case for private capitalism on the concept of property rights, for neither the Constitution nor the 1925 statute was interpreted as an unqualified guarantee of the private ownership of important industries. In reply to repeated questioning regarding the wording of the 1925 Bill, Home Minister Wakatsuji Reijirō stressed that it did not preclude government ownership or control of industry where this was provided for by Diet action. The real objective of the measure, as Wakatsuji took pains to make clear, was to outlaw the Communist Party, which wished to bring about the destruction of the national polity (*kokutai*), and not merely the nationalization of the means of production. See the prolonged debate over this point in the *Shūgiin giji sokkiroku* (50th Session, 1924–25), pp. 327–38, 552–81.

motive be not attacked, but rather purified as it has been in Germany. We believe that the nation should actually encourage profit-making, regardless of how high the rate, if it is just and not contrary either to the aims of business or the objectives of the nation.

The meaning of the term "purified" (*junka*) as applied to the profit motive was not made clear, but the authors of the resolution were obviously seeking to dissociate the pursuit of profit in Japanese business from the self-interested acquisitiveness characteristic of Western capitalism:

The economic world of our country is not merely a transplantation of [economic] liberalism from Europe and America. It is the result of the creativity, ability, effort, and courage of our own businessmen. It has developed organically out of the spirit of the Japanese nation, and has been managed primarily in the interests of the nation. Because this fact is ignored and the idea of *kōeki yūsen* [placing the public interest first] is overly stressed, the world is deliberately given the impression that heretofore the management of enterprises has been motivated entirely by the pursuit of profit.

Specifically, the resolution continued, this false impression resulted from a confusion between the question of what constituted a fair profit (*rijun no tekisei*) and the problem of how profits, once earned, should be distributed (*rieki bunpai no tekisei*). In order to rectify this situation, these business organizations pledged themselves to "shun the unregulated distribution of profits that has prevailed heretofore in the era of a so-called liberal economy, and to distribute profits . . . with the intent of providing for the future development of a sound foundation for enterprise."

The ambivalent manner in which such spokesmen treated the question of profit and incentives reflects the serious dilemma that apologists for private enterprise faced in this period. The traditional themes of self-sacrifice, dedication to the common good, and disdain for private interests were now being used against them by the advocates of a "new economic structure." Yet to abandon these themes in order to place emphasis on the importance of material incentives in the competitive pursuit of profit would have rendered the business class even more vulnerable to charges of selfishness. Business leaders sought a solution to this dilemma in two ways. First, a campaign was launched by Mitsui to convince critics that big business was indeed concerned with the public welfare. Beginning in the early 1930's under the leadership of Ikeda Seihin, Mitsui donated large sums for relief of unemployment and depressed areas. Then in 1933 a special foundation, appropriately called the Mitsui Foundation for the Return of Blessings (Mitsui Hō-on Kai), was created to study possible relief and welfare measures. Stock in Mitsui enterprises was also placed on the public market for the first time, and members of the Mitsui family who had formerly held prominent positions in Mitsui companies retired into the background.[40]

This "camouflage policy," as it was labeled by skeptics, failed to stay the demands for radical economic reform, and the war in China brought increased government intervention in industry and commerce. Finally, in the hope of preserving as much autonomy in private enterprise as possible, business leaders accepted in principle the concept of a new economic structure. The resolution quoted above declared that business groups recognized "the urgent necessity of correcting the evils of the so-called liberal economy" and of "limiting freedom to the extent necessary."[41] By rejecting the principle of economic liberalism, business spokesmen felt free to make certain demands. "The new economic structure must be in accord with those noble qualities peculiar to Japan. It must in no way depart from the concept of *kokutai* [the national polity] or tend toward the destruction of the family system."[42] The president of the Japan Economic Federation explained that in practice, the "new economic structure" ensured that "the people, with their creative initiative, responsibility, and zeal," would still manage enterprises, while the government officials "would serve chiefly to provide overall leadership and supervision, but not direct management."

In the end, the Japanese business elite managed to a surprising degree to maintain independent control of private enterprise. The "new economic structure" established by the promulgation of the Major Industries Association Ordinance in the autumn of 1941 merely extended and tightened the system of cartel control that had been created in the early 1930's at the request of the business community itself. True, the control associations were now brought under the direct supervision of government bureaucrats, but the real power remained in the hands of the directors of the respective control organizations, who were for the most part executives of the leading private companies in each field. Even the special control companies set up in 1943 in the midst of the war to handle the purchase and sale of materials and products for each industry were joint stock companies operating for profit. Despite the elaborate administrative structure that existed on paper during the war years, neither effective centralization nor bureaucratic control was ever fully implemented.[43]

To this extent the business elite won a victory of sorts, but it came after a battle in which the ideological defense of capitalism can hardly be said to have played a significant role. The entrenched economic position of the *zaibatsu* and the dire need for the talents of the private managerial class in the face of a mounting military crisis gave even the most determined opponents of capitalism little alternative but to compromise. Business leaders, for their part, were willing in the end to renounce economic liberalism *in theory* in order to maintain their control over the economy *in practice*. Thus, not even in the 1930's did the Japanese business elite resolve the conflict between the institutional characteristics of private enterprise and the traditional collectivistic ideology upon which their claim to a position of leadership within the society depended. Both the justification of the political and economic power exercised by the private business class and the appeal to labor for harmony and cooperation were based on the premise that Japanese businessmen were unselfishly devoted to the interests of the community as a whole. Yet as Albert O. Hirschman has pointed out in his discussion of contrasting "images" of economic progress, it is precisely because "the idea that the benefits from progress must accrue equally to all" is inherent in the collectivistic orientation that the acquisition of personal wealth or private power is extremely difficult to defend.[44] Western capitalists defended themselves on the grounds that selfishness was the most powerful and efficient motivation for economic endeavor. Japanese capitalists were unable to avail themselves of this type of defense without contradicting the key premises upon which Japanese business ideology was based: that is, they could not extol the profit motive and at the same time claim that they, like the samurai of old, were free of selfishness.

7. Conclusion

We have seen that the ideology of the Japanese business class during the first fifty years of industrialization differed markedly from the capitalist creed of ninteenth- and early twentieth-century England and America. As the authors of *The American Business Creed* point out, the "logical cornerstone" of the classic Anglo-American business ideology is competition.[1] Although ultimate justification for competition between individuals or economic units lies in the social benefit resulting from greater efficiency and the superior goods produced by individuals striving to surpass one another, the motivation to compete is viewed as primarily selfish rather than altruistic. The individual is both guaranteed the right to personal gain and encouraged to employ all his energies and initiative to achieve it. Indeed, income, property, and wealth—the tangible evidence of competitive ability—are the recognized symbols of personal and social success in this view.

Moreover, the classic Anglo-American ideology asserts the natural superiority of the business elite over other elites. The claim that business leaders are entitled to a larger share of prestige, material rewards, and authority within their society is based on three assumptions. First, since social progress is defined in the classic business creed almost exclusively in terms of material progress, the business elite is thought of as the group contributing most directly to the most important goals of society. Secondly, the business world is said to provide a unique testing-ground for natural ability. Unlike the government and other professions, business enterprise pits one individual against another in equal competition, with clearly defined criteria for measuring achievement. Success is determined by the impartial and impersonal workings of a market economy governed by millions of separate choices made by consumers. Finally, private enterprise is justified on the grounds that the institutions of business embody and promote the fundamental values of political freedom and individualism, and are in accord with the natural laws of society, human psychology, and economics.

Spokesmen for the prewar Japanese business elite, by contrast, accepted without apparent reservation the view that individual interests and private gain should be subordinated to the preservation of harmony within an organic society, and rejected the tenets of economic individualism as incompatible with the collectivistic values of Japanese tradition. Competition, in the sense the concept was used in Western capitalist ideology, received only sporadic mention in the early decades of industrialization; and it was not until the 1930's that business leaders attempted to invoke it as an essential prerequisite to economic efficiency, or treat it as a major characteristic of Japanese capitalism. Not even in the 1930's, however, did Japanese business spokesmen make any concerted attempt to justify the profit motive. Their attitude toward material gain in general was basically ambivalent. On the one hand, business leaders stressed the role of modern industry and commerce in achieving material progress—although even here economic development was viewed primarily as a prerequisite to national greatness and only secondarily as a means to material comforts or a higher standard of living for the nation; on the other, material incentives to economic effort were discussed almost exclusively in negative terms, as we have seen in the repeated denials that entrepreneurs were motivated by the desire for personal wealth.

As a corollary to this, Japanese businessmen and their biographers studiously avoided the use of material standards as status symbols or measures of business success.

With the possible exception of Fukuzawa Yukichi, Japanese apologists for private enterprise rarely sought to glorify business as a superior vocation. Although business spokesmen were emphatic in their characterization of business as an honorable means of rendering service to society, and asserted that success in the economic world required dedicated effort, high moral character, and individual ability, their assertions were not accompanied by claims that the business elite were intrinsically superior to others whose success was limited to less demanding fields. It is true that in the Meiji period the modern business class openly demanded a larger voice in the government; but this was justified on the grounds that businessmen were needed to help make intelligent decisions regarding economic issues, and not, as in the classic Anglo-American creed, that business leaders constituted a "natural aristocracy of talent" whose competence extended to all aspects of social life.[2] In other words, the attempt to sanction higher social status for the Meiji entrepreneur was not based on the assertion that business enterprise in itself developed or required peculiar leadership qualities; the claim was rather that involvement in commercial pursuits did not *necessarily* prevent business leaders from emulating the ideal cultural type, the feudal warrior.

What factors shaped Japanese business ideology? Obviously the existence of a hostile tradition in which the open pursuit of self-interest was held in contempt and commerical endeavor was viewed with suspicion placed the Meiji entrepreneur on the defensive. There remains, however, the question of why the business elite did not turn their back on the traditional value system, or attempt to gain acceptance for the types of values emphasized by the capitalist class in the industrial societies of the West. Part of the answer lies in the fact that in the initial stages of industrialization the modern business class in Japan did not find it in their own interest to seek a social consensus radically different from the traditional value system. The existence of an authoritarian government fully committed to industrial development under the sanction of tradition was only one factor favoring the acceptance of these values by the business class. An equally important factor was the social and educational background of Japanese business leaders themselves, which predisposed them to accept the Meiji political orthodoxy. The rejection of the doctrines of economic individualism and Western liberalism put the Meiji business spokesmen in full accord with the intense nationalism of the period, and made possible favorable comparisons between the new entrepreneurs and the traditional samurai elite. Moreover, since the political leaders proved willing, until the 1930's at least, to allow private business considerable freedom, businessmen found little cause for worry concerning the economic role of government.

The themes of patriotic devotion and self-denial in the fulfillment of duty also provided the Meiji industrialist with a defense against critics who sought to better the lot of the working class. Paternalism was a viable approach to labor relations precisely because management could appeal to patriotism and self-sacrifice when arguing that the industrial base was still too narrow and Japan's position vis à vis the West too precarious to permit concessions to labor. So long as the labor force responded to the calls for loyalty and diligence, management had little to lose and much to gain by accepting in principle moral responsibility for the well-being of the working class. By embracing "uniquely Japanese" norms for interpersonal relations in industry, management also found support for its opposition to progressive social legislation modeled on the "foreign" ideals of individual rights and "cash relationships." Finally, circumstances such as the shortage of trained workers often favored the application of paternalistic labor policies in practice. The dictates of economic rationality thus coincided with ideological needs.

Accounting for the remarkable continuity between the ideology of the Meiji entrepreneur and the business class of the

1920's is a more difficult task, but a number of possible causative factors have been suggested. By the 1920's the business elite in Japan had achieved a position that carried with it a considerable measure of power. In view of the economic instability and social turmoil that characterized the decade, it is possible to argue that in the 1920's the business class must have had a greater stake in the status quo than in the alternatives that presented themselves. Since the slogans of Western democracy had been preempted by those most critical of Japanese capitalism, the business elite was reluctant to break with the traditional view of society as an organic whole in which class and individual interests were subordinated to the collective goals of the State. Ironically, the challenge posed by the labor movement in the 1920's, while sufficient to create fear of the consequences of giving in to the demands made on behalf of the working classes, did not develop into a threat adequate to force the adoption of new ideological approaches to industrial relations.

What historical significance can be attached to the type of business ideology that evolved in prewar Japan? In view of Japan's great success at industrialization, the failure to formulate a persuasive rationale for capitalism cannot be said to have hindered the development of economic enterprise. Indeed, the intense nationalism that characterized Japan's response to Western intrusion helped to overcome the barriers to economic progress. Existing studies of Meiji business history indicate that an important factor in accounting for this economic success was the fact that Japanese entrepreneurs were "community-centered" in action as well as in speech.* Future studies may well reveal further evidence that the motives Japanese businessmen claimed as their own may reflect more of reality than their

---

* The term "community-centered" has been coined by Gustav Ranis to describe the motivation of Meiji entrepreneurs, which in Ranis' view was "quasi-tribal, to further the ends of the community; the individual [sought] to grow, not so much in the reflection of his own wealth, a private good, as in the prestige of the cohesive unit, a social good." Ranis, p. 81. Ranis' interpretation is supported by the findings set forth in Hirschmeier.

critics supposed. Their rejection of the theory that economic individualism is essential to economic progress may in retrospect appear to have been justified by what they accomplished in practice.

Nevertheless, Japanese business leaders did fail to convince their critics. The deep-seated hostility that manifested itself so violently in the 1930's, and the recognition by the business elite itself of the dilemma it faced in attempting to justify the private enterprise system testify to this failure. Robert A. Scalapino and others have already suggested some of the broader ramifications of this failure for the political and intellectual history of modern Japan.[3] The Japanese businessman in the prewar period was unable to translate his economic power into sufficient social prestige to allow the type of political claims openly asserted by his counterpart in nineteenth-century England or twentieth-century America. As a result, the business elite continued to occupy a surprisingly weak position in relation to the civil bureaucracy and the military establishment. Yet instead of an *open* alliance with other elements in Japan that sought to use the slogans of Western democracy and parliamentary rule in the competition for political power, "there was a compulsion on the part of the business class to protect and advance its interests secretly, with minimal resort to open political action or democratic procedure."[4] This in turn had serious consequences for the prospects of liberal democracy in prewar Japan, for the ideological conservatism of the business elite was one of the causes of the marked ideological polarization that developed in Japan during the 1920's. At one extreme, the concepts of European Marxism captivated the imaginations of progressive intellectuals, who came to the conclusion that the concentration of economic power in the hands of a conservative capitalist class was the major obstacle to social justice. At the other extreme, the threat of political radicalism led to a reaffirmation of Japan's cultural heritage as a defense against subversive foreign ideas. Caught in the crosscurrents between these two poles, relatively few Japanese held the middle ground where the ideals of individualism and a pluralistic society might have taken root. Instead, traditional symbols were manipulated by ultranationalists and militarists to clear the way for the new authoritarianism of the 1930's.

Placed in this context, an analysis of prewar business ideology sheds light on the puzzling question of how these old values were sustained in the course of a half-century of economic modernization. Explanations of the persistence of traditionalism have stressed two factors as crucial: the role of the State in molding attitudes, particularly through political indoctrination in the schools; and the conservative function of the agrarian village in providing a natural social base for authoritarianism. To these must be added the active part played by the leaders of modern business enterprises who, by adapting traditional norms such as self-abnegation, group solidarity, and paternalistic authority to fit a new industrial context, made a significant contribution to the preservation of the old system of values.

We should not, however, fail to note the tragic irony inherent in such a role. The very ideas advanced by private enterprise in its attempt to justify a position of prestige and power for the modern businessman were wielded as ideological weapons against him in the political struggles of the 1930's. The political parties through which the business community had exerted influence on governmental policy were emasculated; power came to rest in the hands of a coalition of military and civil bureaucrats who almost succeeded in imposing a new economic structure on the nation; and finally, the Imperial Army, having reasserted its own claim as heir to the mantle of the traditional samurai elite, was permitted to gamble away the fruits of seven decades of economic progress.

Notes

Shibusawa Eiichi denki shiryō (*Biographical Materials on Shibusawa Eiichi*), is referred to throughout the Notes as SEDS.

Chapter 1

1. Kerr *et al.*, p. 25. See also Diamond, p. 182.
2. In Tocqueville's phrase, "the lines that divide authority from oppression, liberty from license, and right from might." Quoted from *Democracy in America*, in Bendix, *Work and Authority*, p. 435. I am greatly indebted to Bendix's writings; see his article "Industrialization," and *Nation-Building*.
3. A comprehensive description of this ideology as it is expounded in mid-twentieth century America is contained in Sutton *et al.* Bendix has analyzed its evolution, giving special attention to the problems of labor relations, in *Work and Authority*. Material on various aspects of the subject can be found in Diamond; Hofstadter; Kirkland; Mc-Closky; and Prothro.
4. Pelzel, "The Small Industrialist," p. 90; see also Vogel, p. 160.
5. For discussions and elaborations of this definition of business ideology, see Sutton *et al.*, pp. 1–15, 316–35; Bendix, *Work and Authority*, pp. ix–xxii, 88–89; Bendix, "Industrialization"; Jenks, "Business Ideology."
6. The classical view that the "real" motivation behind all entrepreneurial activity is always the desire to accumulate private wealth or maximize profit has been criticized heavily in recent literature on entrepreneurial behavior: see, for example, Cole, *Business Enterprise*, pp. 15–16, 30–32, 45, 73, 103–8, 234–35; Moore, "The Social Framework of Economic Development," in Braibanti and Spengler, pp. 57–82; Marris, pp. 46–109. For discussions of the motivation of Japanese entrepreneurs in the Meiji period, see Ranis. See also Johannes Hirschmeier, *Origins of Entrepreneurship*.
7. See especially "Industrialization," pp. 617–19, where Bendix defends this approach to the study of ideologies.

8. Scalapino, *Democracy and the Party Movement*, p. 272.

9. Quoted from Yamaga Sokō, in Honjo, *Economic Theory*, p. 26.

10. See Nomura, *Keizai Shisō*, pp. 72–74. Movement did in fact take place between these classes throughout the Tokugawa period. Moreover, toward the end of the period there was growing criticism of the preoccupation with ascribed status in the appointment of officials. As Dore has pointed out, however, the advocates of appointment by merit rarely envisaged the application of this principle to the division of labor within society in general. Their concern was primarily with the criteria for selecting officials from among the samurai class. Dore, *Education*, pp. 186–99.

11. For an excellent discussion of the values of the samurai as seen in their formal education, see Dore, *Education*, pp. 34–64, 301–16. There is also a provocative analysis of the central value system in Bellah, *Tokugawa Religion*, esp. pp. 90–98, 108–13. Bellah's work had been criticized for its exclusive concern with the ideological level in its treatment of Tokugawa values. For our purposes, however, this is not necessarily a shortcoming, since we are concerned primarily with ideology rather than with such questions as the origins of the capitalist spirit in Japan.

12. For an overall view of these developments in English, see Honjo, *Economic Theory*, esp. pp. 34–44, 70–84, 94–110, and 130–34. See also Charles D. Sheldon, pp. 131–43.

13. Quoted from the writings of Satō Shin'en (1769–1850) in Sheldon, p. 134.

14. See the summary of the analysis given by Ogyū Sorai (1666–1728) in McEwan, pp. 35–56.

15. Honjo, p. 97.

16. Quoted from a work by Shingū Ryōtei written in 1828, in Honjo, p. 101.

17. From the excerpts from Muro Kyūsō's *Shundai zatsuwa* [Conversations at Suruga-dai] translated in Tsunoda *et al.*, pp. 439, 441, 442.

18. See the account of the ideas and activities of the Shingaku lecturers in Bellah, *Tokugawa Religion*, pp. 133–76.

19. *Ibid.*, pp. 117–22, 157.

20. Marius B. Jansen, *Sakamoto Ryōma*, pp. 247, 263.

21. From Dazai Shundai, *Sango*, in Takimoto, VI, 350.

22. See Thomas C. Smith, *Political Change*, pp. 13–22; and "Japan's Aristocratic Revolution," pp. 370–83.

23. See Sansom, pp. 476–93; Shively, "Motoda Eifu," pp. 303–33, and "Nishimura Shigeki," pp. 193–241.

24. Quoted in Shibusawa, "Joint Stock Enterprise in Japan," in Okuma, I, 469–70.

25. From the selection from Yamagata's writings reprinted in Tsunoda *et al.*, p. 713.

26. From an editorial in the *Tōyō Keizai Shimpō*, December 25,

1895, pp. 5–8. See also the writings of Fukuzawa Yukichi: for example, the article entitled "Sūchōnin no chii totte kawaru besshi" [Replace the Old Shopkeepers], which appeared in the newspaper *Jiji Shimpō* in 1886, and is reprinted in Fukuzawa Yukichi, *Zenshū*, II, 349–51.

27. *Jitsugyō no Nihon,* August 23, 1897, pp. 29, 30.

Chapter 2

1. In the sense described in Joseph Levenson's brilliant essay, " 'History' and 'Value': The Tensions of Intellectual Choice in Modern China," in Wright, pp. 148–94.

2. I have borrowed the phrase from Rostow, pp. 26–27. For insights into the role of ideologies in the initial stages of industrialization, see Gerschenkron, in Hoselitz, esp. pp. 23–25.

3. See Ienaga, *Gairai bunka,* pp. 148–256. Jansen's *Sakamoto Ryōma* is an excellent account of the life and times of one of the more important of such converts.

4. There is a detailed account of the origins of Meiji government economic policy in Thomas C. Smith, *Political Change.* The existence of a large samurai class, the majority of which were without useful function and quite frequently unable to support the style of life their rank entailed, was also a prime factor in the decision to embark upon industrialization, for industrialization was envisaged as a means of samurai employment.

5. Quoted in Ienaga, *Gairai bunka,* p. 260.

6. See Thomas C. Smith, *Political Change,* for an account of government efforts in the crucial first decade. Lockwood, *Economic Development of Japan,* gives the most thorough overall survey of the role of the government; see especially Chap. 10, pp. 499–592.

7. The "Memorial on the Promotion of Industry," submitted to the Dajōkan in May 1874, *Okubo Toshimichi monjo,* IV, 561–64. The Memorial is also summarized in Sidney D. Brown, p. 190, and in Iwata, pp. 237–38.

8. From the "Opinion Paper on the Establishment of a Steel Works" (undated, ca. 1890), in Itō Hirobumi, *Jitsugyō kōgyō shiryō,* pp. 70–74.

9. From the government announcement of the establishment of the Tomioka filature. Reprinted in Inoue Kaoru Kō Denki Hensankai, II, 458.

10. *Ibid.,* p. 459; also quoted in Thomas C. Smith, *Political Change,* p. 59. For another example of the denial that the government intended to compete with the people, see Shōkō Gyōseishi Kankokai, I, 51–52.

11. See the quotations in Thomas C. Smith, *Political Change,* p. 26.

12. This document can be found in Okuma, *Okuma monjo,* II, 138–49.

13. Godai, pp. 448, 449.

14. March 25, 1898, p. 6.

15. Petition submitted in January 1899 by the Nagoya Chamber of Commerce, reprinted in *Nagoya Shōkō Kaigisho*, II, 121.

16. Petition submitted in 1900, reprinted in *Osaka Shōkō Kaigisho*, p. 68.

17. See, for instance, Fine, pp. 97–98, 111–13. For an interesting study of the "myth" of *laissez-faire* and the role of state governments in the American economy during the first half of the nineteenth century, see Louis Hartz, esp. pp. 287–320.

18. Quoted in Thomas C. Smith, *Political Change*, p. 95.

19. Tokutomi, II, 466–72, 556; see also *Nihon tetsudōshi*, II, 797–830. There is a lengthy study in English by a former Assistant Councilor of the Imperial Board of Railways, Watarai Toshiharu, titled "Nationalization of Railways in Japan," in *Studies in History, Economics and Public Law*, The Faculty of Political Science of Columbia University, LXIII, 2 (1915), 189–339.

20. SEDS, XIX, 664–68; XXI, 356–65 and 713–17; *Osaka Shōkō Kaigisho*, p. 451; *Nagoya Shōkō Kaigisho*, Part I, pp. 320–22. The businessmen of Nagoya, then still relatively isolated from the major urban markets of Osaka and Tokyo, were particularly interested in the development of transportation facilities; see *Nagoya Shōkō Kaigisho*, Part II, pp. 35–36, 104–5, and 151–52.

21. SEDS, XIX, 666.

22. See Shibusawa's article in the August 30, 1898, issue of *Jiji Shimpō*; reprinted in SEDS, XXI, 364–65.

23. The speech is reprinted in its entirety in Tsubotani, pp. 42–56.

24. Article in *Tōyō Keizai Shimpō*, February 15, 1908, p. 206.

25. Interview in *Jitsugyō no Nihon*, August 23, 1897, pp. 37–38.

26. Speech before the 22d Session of the House of Representatives, March 17, 1906; reprinted in *Shimada*, I, 295.

27. See the Tokyo Chamber of Commerce petition of 1898; SEDS, XXI, 358–59.

28. See his article in *Jitsugyō no Nihon*, January 1898, pp. 10–12.

29. See, for example, the 1898 petition submitted to the government by the Tokyo Chamber of Commerce. Fujiyama Raita, who initiated the petition, protested that the government-owned factories were producing a wide variety of goods, many of which were nonmilitary in character, and thereby were hindering the growth of private enterprise; SEDS, XXI, 737–39.

30. See Miyamoto Mataji, *Kabunakama no kenkyū*; and Sheldon.

31. Quoted from an Osaka ordinance of 1872 in Miyamoto Mataji, *Nihon no girudo no kaihō*, pp. 27–28.

32. *Ibid.*, pp. 37–42.

33. See the memorial reprinted in *Okuma monjo*, II, 138–49.

34. *Osaka Shōkō Kaigisho*, pp. 9–10; also Godai, pp. 434ff.

35. The relevant portions of the *Tōkyō Shōkō Kaigisho yōken-*

roku [The Records of the Tokyo Chamber of Commerce] are reprinted in SEDS, XVII, 112–21.

36. *Ibid.*, pp. 112–13.

37. For the view of an influential government bureaucrat, see Maeda Masana, *Kōgyō iken* [Views on Promoting Industry], reprinted in Ouchi and Tsuchiya, XVIII, 82–83.

38. Reprinted from the March 15, 1879, issue in Ouchi and Tsuchiya, p. 122.

39. SEDS, XVIII, 140ff.

40. For these discussions, see the excerpts from the *Kangyōkai, Kōmubu nisshi* [Proceedings of the Section on Industry of the Conference on the Encouragement of Industry], in SEDS, XVIII, 159ff. For similar views expressed in 1899 in support of stricter enforcement of the regulations for *dōgyō kumiai*, see *Nagoya Shōkō Kaigisho*, Part II, pp. 123–24.

41. See Shōkō Gyōseishi Kankokai, I, 272–74.

42. SEDS, XVIII, 359–79.

43. Cf. Scalapino, *Democracy*, pp. 271–72.

Chapter 3

1. Adam Smith, pp. 421–23.

2. Hofstadter, esp. pp. 18–36.

3. Quoted in Diamond, pp. 62–63.

4. Quoted in Bendix, *Work and Authority*, p. 257. For other discussions of self-interest, the profit motive, and the philosophy of economic individualism, see Sutton *et al.*, pp. 168–71, 254–56, 351–56; Schlatter, pp. 239–77; and Prothro, pp. 96–107.

5. Quoted from *"Beiō kairan jiki"* ("Report on Travels through America and Europe"), in Ienaga, *Dōtoku shisōshi*, p. 243.

6. The best overall view of Fukuzaka's thought available in either English or Japanese can be found in Blacker. There is a good survey of his economic ideas in Sumiya Etsuji, pp. 72–91.

7. Quoted from *"Seiyō jijō gaihen"* ("Conditions in the West: Supplementary Volume"), published in 1867 in Sumiya Etsuji, *Nihon keizaigaku shi*, p. 83.

8. Fukuzawa Yukichi, *Fukuō hyakuwa*, p. 152. These discourses were first published as articles in Fukuzawa's newspaper *Jiji Shimpō*, in 1896.

9. *Ibid.*, p. 153.

10. There is a good discussion of Taguchi in Sumiya Etsuji, *Nihon keizaigaku shi*, pp. 129–50, esp. pp. 142–44. See also Kada, pp. 380–92.

11. See, for example, Fukuzawa, *Fukuō hyakuwa*, pp. 49–50, 66–68, 138–40.

12. Nishihara, pp. 141–42. Also quoted in Kajinishi, p. 239.

13. Shibusawa came to be regarded as the personification of the

ideal of the patriotic entrepreneur; see the pages devoted to him in the textbooks for moral education translated in Hall, pp. 194–95.

14. "Jinseikan" ("My View of Life"), in Shibusawa, *Seien hyakuwa,* p. 2.

15. "Dokuritsu jiei" ("Independence and Self-reliance"), *ibid.,* p. 542.

16. *Ibid.,* pp. 539–40.

17. *Ibid.,* p. 543.

18. Wakamiya, p. 139, 158–59.

19. Wada, p. 303; also quoted in Tsuchiya, *Keieisha seishin,* p. 219. This work by Tsuchiya includes interesting studies of Shibusawa, Morimura, Kinbara, and two other Meiji entrepreneurs.

20. Wakamiya, p. 20.

21. Quoted from an interview in the October 10, 1908 issue of the business journal *Jitsugyō no Nihon,* in Suzuki Gorō, pp. 261–62. See also pp. 214–16.

22. Godai, p. 595.

23. Said of Okura Kihachirō in the August 1898 issue of the *Jitsugyō no Nihon,* p. 39.

24. Preface contributed by Matsukata Kojirō, president of the Kawasaki Shipbuilding Company, in Asano and Asano, p. 22. See also Fujiyama Raita's comment, *ibid.,* p. 36.

25. Comment by Magoshi Kyohei in Onishi, *Asabuki Eiji,* Appendix, p. 66. Similar comments can be found in many biographies of Japanese businessmen: see for further examples Nakarai, p. 890; Mitsuoka, pp. 487–93; Itsukakai, Appendix, p. 10.

26. Quoted in Tsuchiya, *Keieisha seishin,* p. 276.

27. Wakamiya, p. 20. See also pp. 146–47.

28. *Ibid.,* p. 17. See also Shibusawa's remarks on the reasons why many businesses fail, *Seien hyakuwa,* pp. 241–49.

29. Tokutomi, II, 718–24. For similar stories of patriotic decisions, see Hirschmeier, *Origins of Entrepreneurship,* pp. 221, 234, 237. It is true that in most such stories patriotic motivation ends in business success and presumably in profit, though profit is rarely mentioned. One reader has pointed out that this seems very much like the Invisible Hand in reverse: those who seek the good of society will be assured wealth by a moralistic Providence. Yet it is clear that the emphasis in the statements quoted is on the readiness to sacrifice rather than on material rewards for good works. The logic of this view becomes clearer when the concept of "spiritual compensation" is introduced.

30. The statement is by Morimura Ichizaemon, quoted in Wakamiya, p. 162.

31. From a speech given at the Fall 1905 meeting of the Nihonsha (The Japan Society); reprinted in SEDS, XXIII, 662–66.

32. A translation of this selection from Shibusawa, *Seien hyakuwa* is given in Obata, pp. 266–70.

33. *Ibid.*, pp. 267–68. See also the discourses entitled "Rongo to soroban" ("The Analects and the Abacus"), and "Bushidō to jitsugyō" ("Bushidō and Business"), in Shibusawa, *Seien hyakuwa,* pp. 196–203, 274–75.

34. From a speech to the 1907 meeting of the Shakai Seisaku Gakkai (Association for the Study of Social Policy); Shakai Seisaku Gakkai, *Kōjōhō to rōdō mondai,* p. 46. The speech is also reprinted in SEDS, XXVII, 370–71.

35. *Ibid.*, pp. 46–51.

36. Obata, pp. 136–37.

37. "Agricultural Improvement in Japan: 1870–1900," in *Economic Development and Cultural Change,* IX, Part II (October 1960), 87.

38. Quoted in Fairbank *et al.*, p. 540.

39. *Jitsugyō no Nihon,* January 1900, p. 34.

40. *Tōyō Keizai Shimpō,* December 5, 1905, pp. 1562–65.

41. Dore, p. 41.

42. Kaneko related the story to make the point that even he himself had not fully overcome his prejudices at the time; Hara, I, 217–18; see also p. 6. It is interesting to note that Hara, who became a very important figure in financial circles, had given up the idea of a government career partly because he believed it impossible to climb very high in the bureaucracy without being a member of one of the powerful cliques. No doubt this was an important factor in the decisions of other men, e.g., Shibusawa and Godai, to leave government positions for business. See also Kataoka, pp. 76–77.

43. Godai, p. 252. See also pp. 228–29.

44. Asano and Asano, p. 23.

45. These ties are discussed in Scalapino, pp. 260–62, and in Ike, pp. 96–98. See also the description of the intimate relationship between Inoue Kaoru and Mitsui and other business firms in Inoue Kaoru Kō Denki Hensankai, IV, 154–224, 662–726.

46. The Keishin Club was formed by Okura Kihachirō, Masuda Takashi, and Shibusawa Eiichi in May 1889; SEDS, XXIII, 5–21. A year earlier, the Jiji Kenkyūkai (The Society for the Study of Local Self-Government) was organized as part of an abortive plan by Inoue Kaoru to form a conservative political party composed of "men of means of the middle class or higher"; see Inoue Kaoru Kō Denki Hansankai, II, 434–38. These organizations were merely the first of a long line of business groups concerned with political issues.

47. SEDS, XXIII, 22–26. The list of participants included such prominent business figures as Okura, Masuda, Yasuda Zenjirō, Amamiya Keijirō, Magoshi Kyohei, and Hara Rokurō.

48. Computed from the table in *Nihon kindaishi jiten,* pp. 766–67. The figures include those members of the Lower House who listed their occupations as banking, commerce, industry, or mining, or who

called themselves "company employees," regardless of the size or locale of their enterprises. See also Scalapino, pp. 254–56.

49. *Jitsugyō no Nihon,* February 15, 1898, pp. 1–2. Even without revision of the election laws, the election of 1898 resulted in an increase of some 16 "business" representatives, bringing the total to almost 19 per cent of the Lower House. Business groups were still unsatisfied, however; see, for example, the petition of the Nagoya Chamber of Commerce, submitted to the Diet in January 1899, and reprinted in *Nagoya Shōkō Kaigisho,* Part II, p. 121.

50. SEDS, XXIII, 42.

51. February 5, 1900, pp. 1–6.

52. *Ibid.*

53. From a speech to a meeting of the Shōkō Keizai Kai reprinted in SEDS, XXIII, 97–98.

54. The term "jitsugyōka" was coined by Shibusawa Eiichi as part of this conscious effort to create a new image and to distinguish the Meiji business elite from the merchant of the past; see Hirschmeier, pp. 172–73.

55. Interview with Otani Kahei in the *Tōyō Keizai Shimpō,* April 15, 1896, p. 15. See also Shibusawa's argument in 1910 that Japan must make preparations because America's stated purpose was "a peaceful war—i.e., a commercial war"; *Seien hyakuwa,* pp. 701–2.

56. *Tōyō Keizai Shimpō,* December 1896.

57. Morimura Ichizaemon, address at the Waseda School of Business, April 15, 1905, reprinted in the May 15, 1905 issue of *Tōyō Keizai Shimpō,* pp. 635–36.

58. Editorial in the *Tōyō Keizai Shimpō,* November 15, 1895.

59. Jiji Tsūshinsha Henshukyoku, p. 18.

60. Quoted from the May 1889 issue of *Ryūmon Zasshi,* in Hirschmeier, p. 170.

61. *Tōkai Keizai Shimpō,* August 1880.

62. *Ibid.*

63. Editorial in the December 25, 1895 issue, pp. 5–8. See also the series of articles on leading businessmen that appeared in the *Jitsūgyo no Nihon,* especially those on Okura Kihachirō in the August 1898 issue, pp. 36–38; and on Yasuda Zenjirō in the April 1898 issue, pp. 45–48.

64. As recalled by Kaneko Kentarō in Hara, I, 218.

65. Wada, p. 293.

66. Wakamiya, p. 146; see also Uzaki, pp. 369–72.

67. Quoted from an article in an 1896 issue of the *American Journal of Sociology* in Bendix, *Work and Authority,* p. 256.

Chapter 4

1. This account is based on the excerpts from the *Tōkyō Shōhō Kaigisho yōkenroku,* reprinted in SEDS, XVII, 480–90, 533–42.

2. SEDS, XVIII, 102–8. The government had begun drafting such a law in 1882; Kazahaya, pp. 117–18.

3. The proceedings of this conference are reprinted in part in SEDS, XVIII, 121–34.

4. *Ibid.*, p. 117.

5. The details of the debate over labor legislation in Meiji Japan are related in Kazahaya and in Kishimoto. Although reliable in most respects, neither presents a very objective account of the problem. It is necessary to go to the primary sources in order to gain a more balanced view.

6. Kazahaya, p. 117.

7. The *Daiikkai Nōshōkō Kōtōkaigi giji sokkiroku* (The Stenographic Records of the Proceedings of the First Plenary Conference on Agriculture, Commerce and Industry) are reprinted in part in SEDS, XXIII, 492–580. The portions relating to the proposed labor laws are also available in *Meiji bunka shiryō*, I, 17–57.

8. From the statement by Soeda Jūichi, a high-ranking official of the Ministry; SEDS, XXIII, 512.

9. SEDS, XXIII, 492.

10. *Ibid.*, p. 514.

11. The Proceedings of the 3d Conference on Agriculture, Commerce, and Industry (1898), reprinted in *Meiji bunka shiryō*, I, 104–7. The speaker was Shimura Genjirō, then chief of the Bureau of Industry (Kōgyōkyoku) of the Ministry of Agriculture and Commerce. Two years later, while vice-president of the Kangyō Bank, Shimura wrote an article in which he suggested that large-scale organization of industry was not desirable, so serious were the labor problems it engendered. It was his opinion that efforts should be made instead to maintain small industrial units; "Kōgyō shiki to rōdō mondai" ("Industrial Organization and the Labor Problem"), in *Tōyō Keizai Shimpō*, no. 127 (1900), pp. 110–12. Additional examples of this assumption concerning the inevitable effects of industrialization can be found in Sumiya Mikio, *Nihon chinrōdō shiron*, pp. 298–325.

12. See, e.g., the speech by the Minister of Agriculture and Commerce introducing the Factory Bill to the House of Representatives on February 2, 1910; *Dainijūrokkai Teikoku Gikai Shūgiin giji sokkiroku* (The Stenographic Records of the Proceedings of the 26th Session of the House of Representatives of the Imperial Diet), pp. 83–85. See also the hearings of the Committee on the Factory Bill in *Dainijūshichi Teikoku Gikai Shūgiin iinkai kaigiroku*; and Kishimoto, pp. 130–44.

13. SEDS, XXIII, 527.

14. See his speech to the 1907 conference of the Association for the Study of Social Policy in Shakai Seisaku Gakkai, eds., *Kōjōhō to rōdō mondai*, p. 50.

15. SEDS, XVIII, 118, 124.

16. SEDS, XXIII, 530.

17. Quoted from an article in the *Tōyō Keizai Shimpō* by Kaza-haya, p. 126.

18. A concise description of the labor movement prior to 1911 can be found in Okochi, *Reimeiki no nihon rōdō undō*; see also Sumiya Mikio, *Nihon chinrōdō shiron*, pp. 269–325. Brief accounts in English can be found in Okochi, *Labor in Modern Japan*, and in Scalapino, "Japan," pp. 75–145.

19. Dan expressed this view in an interview reported in the December 15, 1897 issue of the *Jitsugyō no Nihon*, pp. 31–32.

20. From the monthly report of the Tokyo Chamber of Commerce for November 1898; reprinted in SEDS, XXI, 345–46.

21. *Nagoya Shōkō Kaigisho*, Part II, p. 143.

22. Interview reported in the *Tōyō Keizai Shimpō*, February 25, 1908, p. 254.

23. Quoted in Kanda, p. 5.

24. *Nagoya Shōkō Kaigisho*, Part II, p. 143.

25. See the speech before the Lower House by Tanabe Kumaichi, March 1909, *Dai Nihon Teikoku Gikai shi* (The Records of the Imperial Diet), VII, 1100–1101.

26. *Tōyō Keizai Shimpō*, February 25, 1908, pp. 254–55.

27. Quoted from a speech by Viscount Watanabe Kunitake, one of the founders of the Seiyūkai party, in Kanda, pp. 3–4.

28. SEDS, XVIII, 126.

29. *Ibid.*, XXI, 346.

30. From a statement by Okada Taizo before the February 17, 1911 session of the Committee on the Factory Bill; *Dainijūshichi Teikoku Gikai Shugiin iinkai kaigiroku* (the Minutes of the Committee Proceedings of the 27th Session of the House of Representatives), "Kōjōhōan Kaikiroku," p. 11.

31. Quoted in Kanda, p. 5.

32. *Nagoya Shōkō Kaikisho*, Part II, p. 116.

33. There are general accounts of this trend in Sansom, pp. 384–94; and Delmar M. Brown, pp. 112–47. Details of various aspects can be found in Kōsaka Masaaki, ed., *Japanese Thought*, pp. 210–61, 360–91; and Warren W. Smith, Jr., *Confucianism*, pp. 55–102. Dore has offered some insights into the specific importance of the institution of the family in this context in his *City Life in Japan*, pp. 91–96.

34. See the 1898 statement by the Tokyo Chamber of Commerce: SEDS, XXI, 346.

35. From an article in Okuma, I, 129.

36. The nature of the problem of obedience and efficiency in industrial relations has been treated at length in Bendix's *Work and Authority*; see also the concise summary in his article, "Managerial Ideologies" in *Economic Development and Cultural Change*, V, 2 (January 1957), 118–28.

37. There are several interesting studies in English that treat paternalistic practices in postwar Japan: e.g., Abegglen; Bennett and

Iwao; and Levine, *Industrial Relations.* See also the discussion of "administrative paternalism" in Ballon. Unfortunately, however, relatively little attention has been paid to the historical development of present labor practices, and there is as yet no thorough study of prewar managerial policies available in either English or Japanese. The most ambitious attempt to fill this gap is made by Hazama. In English, there is a brief outline of the subject by Sakurabayashi and Ballon, "Labor-Management Relations in Modern Japan: A Historical Survey of Personnel Administration," in Roggendorf, pp. 245–66; see also Levine's brief survey of the evolution of the Japanese wage structure, "Labor Markets and Collective Bargaining in Japan," in Lockwood, *The State and Economic Enterprise in Japan,* pp. 633–67.

38. See Bendix, *Work and Authority,* pp. 46–116.

39. For studies of some of the more important enterprises in such key industries as cotton spinning, mining, and shipbuilding, see Hazama.

40. The importance of the character of Japanese farming and the environment of village life has been discussed at length in Thomas C. Smith, *Agrarian Origins;* see especially pp. 210–13. For another penetrating analysis of "holistic" and "submissive" attitudes and their persistence in rural Japan, see Dore, *Land Reform,* pp. 385–404.

41. Okochi, pp. 2–3.

42. Sumiya Mikio, *Nihon chinrōdō shiron,* Table 12, p. 114.

43. Computed from Table vi in International Labour Organization, *Industrial Labour in Japan,* p. 24.

44. *Ibid.,* Table iv, p. 22; see also Kazahaya, Table 3, p. 156.

45. Computed from International Labour Organization, *Industrial Labour in Japan,* Table v, p. 23; see also Kazahaya, Table 7, p. 160.

46. For a good description of this type of labor-management relations in a small factory in postwar Kyoto, see Olson, Chapter 2.

47. Sumiya Mikio, *Nihon chinrōdō shiron,* Table 12, p. 114.

48. Kishimoto, p. 45; see also *Industrial Labour in Japan,* Table vi, p. 24.

49. Sumiya Mikio, *Nihon chinrōdō shiron,* pp. 203–7; Shindo, pp. 36–39, 86–89; and Sakurabayashi and Ballon, p. 250.

50. See Sumiya Mikio, *Nihon chinrōdō shiron,* pp. 140–42.

51. Morita Yoshio, pp. 36–45; see also Sumiya Mikio, *Nihon chinrōdō shiron,* pp. 194–95.

52. International Labour Office, *Industrial Labour in Japan,* pp. 84–85.

53. Onishi, *Asabuki Eiji,* pp. 193–209; and Mutō, I, 85–89. The refusal of Kanegafuchi to subscribe to the labor agreements of the Kansai spinner group led in 1896 to a violent dispute between the two that was only settled after a number of prominent government and business figures had intervened (Onishi, *Asabuki Eiji,* p. 209, and Mutō, I, 91–95).

54. Interview with Hatano Shōgorō, an executive of the Mitsui Bank, in the *Tōyō Keizai Shimpō*, April 15, 1907, pp. 460–61.

55. See Sumiya Mikio, *Nihon chirōdō shiron*, pp. 203–7; Shindo, pp. 36–39, 86–89; and Sakurabayashi and Ballon, p. 246n.

56. Quoted in Itsukakai, pp. 272–73.

57. Yamaguchi Kisaburo Den Hensan Iinkai, pp. 26–27. Yamaguchi, who received the Ph.D. degree from Johns Hopkins University, was to become a prominent figure in the business world as president of the Tokyo Shibaura Electric Company.

58. Sakurabayashi and Ballon, pp. 250–51; see also Solomon Levine, "Labor Markets" pp. 642–48; and Hazama, p. 39n.

59. Sakurabayashi and Ballon, pp. 249–50. The *oyakata* system was retained in its traditional form in such industries as construction and lumbering; see Bennett and Iwao for a very interesting description of this pre-Meiji labor institution.

60. The concern on the part of management over the shortage of skilled labor, particularly in the period of rapid economic expansion following the outbreak of the Russo-Japanese War, is amply attested to by the repeated pleas for increased government aid to education found in the pages of such economic journals as the *Tōyō Keizai Shimpō* and in the petitions from the various local Chambers of Commerce.

61. Shukuri, pp. 524–30.

62. See the *Tōyō Keizai Shimpō*, July 25, 1905, pp. 948–49.

63. See Sumiya Mikio, "Shakai undō," in Ienaga *et al.*, XVIII, 153–96.

64. See Solomon Levine's comments on conformity to the purposes of the collectivity, in *Industrial Relations*, pp. 36–37.

65. Itsukakai, p. 116. See also Iwasaki Yatarō's speeches to Mitsubishi employees quoted in Shukuri, pp. 25–29.

66. Sumiya Mikio, "Kokuminteki," in Ito Yoshi *et al.*, V, 25–26n. Ninomiya's teachings are described in Bellah, *Tokugawa Religion*, pp. 126–31. For other references to Ninomiya's ideas by Japanese businessmen, see Makino Motojirō, *Taiken zaigo*, p. 180; and Tanaka, pp. 1–4.

67. Kawai Tetsuo, pp. 252–53.

68. From a letter by Hirose Saihei to Iba Teigo dated March 1895, reprinted in Nishikawa, p. 158. See also the reminiscences of the Sumitomo executive Ogura Masatane, *Ogura Masatane dansō*, pp. 123–26, 196.

69. Takahashi Shinkichi, article in the *Jitsugyō no Nihon*, March 1912, p. 4.

70. Koyama Kenzō, article in the *Jitsugyō no Nihon*, June 1898, p. 12.

71. Interview in the *Jitsugyō no Nihon*, February 1899, pp. 36–39; see also the remarks on ambition in the article "Yasuda Zenjirō

o ronsu" (A Discussion of Yasuda Zenjirō), *Jitsugyō no Nihon,* April 1898, pp. 45–48.

72. Shibusawa, *Seien hyakuwa,* pp. 348, 353.

73. Sumiya Mikio, "Shakai undō," p. 189; also Kishimoto, pp. 136–37.

74. Tsurumi, III, 201–2. See the excerpts from his speeches to workers, pp. 208–12; also Shibusawa's discussion of the family and economic enterprises, *Seien hyakuwa,* pp. 605–16.

75. Makino Ryōzō, II, 186. Nakahashi retired to devote full time to politics in 1914. He later served as Minister of Education in the Seiyūkai Cabinets (1919–22), as Minister of Commerce under Tanaka Giichi (1927–29), and finally as Home Minister (1931–32).

76. Reprinted in *Fukuzawa Yukichi Zenshū,* VI, 448. It is also quoted in Kada, p. 763.

77. SEDS, XXIII, 520. Also quoted in Kazahaya, p. 128.

78. *Nagoya Shōkō Kaigisho,* Part II, p. 143.

79. Kanda, pp. 4–5; also Kazahaya, p. 129.

80. See the hearings of the Committee on the Factory Bill of the House of Representatives, in *Dainijūshichi Teikoku Gikai Shūgiin iinkai kaigiroku.*

81. Contrast the American business reaction to outside interference in the determination of working conditions, in Fine, pp. 104–6; Bendix, *Work and Authority,* pp. 267–69. Contrast also the vigorous rearguard action against "collectivistic" social legislation in England, in Ausubel, pp. 41–47, 122–35.

82. Interview reported in the April 25, 1907 issue of *Tōyō Keizai Shimpō,* p. 558; see also Shōda's article in the December 25, 1900 issue, pp. 1684–86. Other examples of such arguments can be found, especially in Taguchi Ukichi's journal, *Tōkyō Keizai Zasshi,* where he consistently maintained a laissez-faire position.

83. Interview in the March 5, 1910 *Tōyō Keizai Shimpō,* pp. 321–22.

Chapter 5

1. See the chapter by Allen, "The Concentration of Economic Control," in Schumpeter, pp. 625–46.

2. See, for example, the editorial entitled "Daisen no motaseru shisō no henka" (The Changes in Thought Brought about by the World War) in *Tōyō Keizai Shimpō,* November 25, 1918, pp. 688–89.

3. There is a very good treatment of Suzuki's life and thought in Nakamura Katsunori, "Suzuki Bunji," in *Hōgaku Kenkyū,* Vol. XXXII, Nos. 1, 2, 3, and 6 (January, February, and June 1959), pp. 43–67, 139–63, and 481–510. See also Suzuki's own *Rōdō undō nijūnen.*

4. Nakamura Katsunori, p. 58. For Shibusawa's role in gaining permission for Suzuki to go abroad, see the letter from Sidney L. Gulick reprinted in Obata, pp. 297–98; also the 1918 article by Shibusawa reprinted in SEDS, XXXI, 609.

5. Quoted from an essay written in 1918, in Sumiya Mikio, "Rōdō undō," in Itō Yoshi *et al.*, V, 189.

6. Quoted from an article in the November 1914 issue of the Yūaikai organ *Rōdō oyobi Sangyō*, in Nakamura Katsunori, pp. 144–45.

7. Quoted from the October 1916 issue of the *Rōdō oyobi Sangyō*, p. 57.

8. Quoted from Suzuki Bunji, *Nihon no rōdō mondai* (Labor Problems in Japan), published in 1918: in Sumiya, "Rōdō undō," p. 192.

9. For surveys in English of the left-wing social and political movements of the 1920's, see Scalapino, *Democracy*, pp. 297–345; also Swearingen and Langer, pp. 3–58.

10. The following table is from Kyōchōkai, *Saikin no shakai undō*, p. 323:

	1915	1916	1917	1918
Number of disputes ...	64	108	398	417
Workers involved	7,852	8,413	57,309	66,457

11. *Ibid.*, p. 734; see also International Labour Office, p. 82. The details of the origins, objectives, and membership of the Industrial Club can be found in Nakamura Mototada, I, 1–37.

12. *Ibid.*, pp. 25–26.

13. Shibusawa's major speeches and published statements relating to the labor problem in the years 1912–26 have been reprinted in SEDS, XXXI, 605–62.

14. "Kyū shujū dōtoku no hassan," reprinted from the December 1917 issue of the magazine *Chūō Kōron*, in *ibid.*, pp. 625–26.

15. In addition to Shibusawa, the idea had the support of Kiyoura Keigo, Home Minister Tokonami Takejirō, President of the House of Peers Tokugawa Iesato, and Speaker of the House of Representatives Ooka Ikuzō. Kyōchōkai, *Saikin no shakai undō*, pp. 991–92.

16. Nakamura Mototada, I, 133.

17. *Ibid.*, p. 134.

18. The functions and purposes of the Kyōchōkai are described in Kyōchōkai, *Saikin no shakai undō*, pp. 991–99; and in Kyōchōkai, *Kyōchōkai jigyō ippan*.

19. Kyōchōkai, *Saikin no shakai undō*, p. 994.

20. See the denial by Kawamura Takeji, Director of the Police Bureau of the Home Ministry, that amendment of the Peace Preservation Law was necessary: *Tōyō Keizai Shimpō*, April 5, 1919, pp. 569–70. A survey of the laws affecting labor organizations prior to 1919 can be found in Kyōchōkai, *Saikin no shakai undō*, pp. 741–43.

21. See the articles and speeches reprinted in SEDS, XXXI, 610–20.

22. Kyōchōkai, *Saikin no shakai undō*, pp. 816–24. See also Kazahaya, *Shakai seisakushi*, pp. 351–62; and Kishimoto, *Shakai seisaku shi*, pp. 179–82.

23. Kyōchōkai, *Saikin no shakai undō*, pp. 818–20.

24. "Onjō Shugi o motte rōdō mondai o kaiketsu" (Let Us Solve the Labor Problem by Means of Onjō Shugi), *Jitsugyō no Nihon*, April 15, 1919, pp. 11–15.

25. Mishima Yakichi, president of the San'eki Shōkai Company, in "I Advocate San'eki Shugi," *Jitsugyō no Nihon*, April 15, 1919, p. 22.

26. Morita, p. 133. See also the statement by the Industrial Club president, Dan Takuma, in *ibid.*, pp. 133–34.

27. As translated from Mutō's article in the magazine *Daiyamondo*, in the *Japan Financial and Economic Monthly*, October 1919, p. 21.

28. Morita, p. 144.

29. Nakamura Mototada, I, 490.

30. *Japan Financial and Economic Monthly*, October 1919, p. 21.

31. From the "Statement of the Committee to Study Means of Maintaining Peace in Industry of the Kantō Association of Industrial Organizations" ["Kantō Sangyō Dantai Rengōkai"], March 1934; quoted in Morita, Appendix III, p. 418.

32. Nakamura Mototada, I, 489; II, 704.

33. *Ibid.*, II, 705.

34. Ko Dan Danshaku Kenki Hensan Iinkai, *Danshaku Dan*, II, 77.

35. Nakamura Mototada, I, 495; see the similar arguments in the opinion submitted by the Nagoya Chamber of Commerce in 1925, *Nagoya Shōkō Kaigisho*, Part II, p. 330.

36. Nakamura Mototada, I, 492. Pamphlets addressed to the workers repeated these charges, and also accused union organizers of bullying tactics and acts of terrorism; Rōmu Kondankai, eds., *Rōdōsha shokun ! naze zenkoku jitsugyōka dantai wa rōdō kumiai hōan ni hantai shita ka* (Workers! Why Have Business Groups throughout the Country Opposed the Labor Union Bill?), n.p.

37. International Labour Office, *Industrial Labour in Japan,* Table V, p. 23.

38. *Ibid.*, Table III, p. 21. A large number of these females were employed in textile mills; but the important position of women in the industrial sector as a whole is indicated by the fact that they comprised some 50 per cent of the work force in all types of factories utilizing prime movers; *ibid.*, Table VI, p. 24.

39. See Levine, "Labor Markets," pp. 645–51.

40. Statistics on the education of workers are given in Hazama, p. 62. For an analysis of the social values taught in primary schools,

136 / *Notes to pp. 92–96*

see Kawashima, pp. 40–44, 48–50. Some companies sought to continue the moral education their workers had received in school by sponsoring special lectures on patriotism, ethics, and even religion; see, for example, Ogura, p. 69.

41. For a penetrating comment on the ideology of American businessmen, see Key, p. 77.

42. See Okochi, p. 45.

43. One indication of the increased political influence of private businessmen as a class can be seen in the proportion of members of the Lower House who gave their occupation as "commerce" or "industry": it rose from a fifth of the total membership in 1908 to a third in 1924 (computed from the table in *Nihon kindaishi jiten*, p. 767). Furthermore, among the more prominent political figures of the 1920's were such men as Hara Kei, who served as director of the Furukawa Mining Company before becoming Prime Minister in 1918; Katō Kōmei, son-in-law of the head of the Mitsubishi family, Iwasaki Yanosuke, and Prime Minister from 1924 to 1925; Yamamoto Tatsuo, the Seiyūkai party leader who had spent his early career with Mitsubishi; Yamamoto Tetsujirō, onetime Mitsui executive; and Nakahashi Tokugorō, former president of the Osaka Shipping Company.

44. For a discussion of the importance of this alliance to the Anti-Corn Law League, and its effect on the development of the ideology of the English business class, see Bendix, *Work and Authority*, pp. 100–108.

Chapter 6

1. For an account of the history of the Association, see Sumiya Etsuji, *Nihon keizaigakushi no issetsu*. The proceedings of the annual conferences from 1907 to 1921 have been published by the Association in a series entitled *Shakai Seisaku Gakkai ronsō*.

2. There is a good description of Kanai's career and ideas in Kawai Eijirō's *Meiji shisōshi no ichi dammen*.

3. Sumiya Etsuji, *Nihon keizaigakushi no issetsu*, pp. 262–64.

4. Shakai Seisaku Gakkai, *Kōjōhō to rōdō mondai*, p. 1.

5. Quoted in Sumiya Etsuji, *Nihon keizaigakushi no issetsu*, p. 264.

6. Kuwada, *Shakai seisaku*, pp. 10–14; see also Sumiya Etsuji, *Nihon keizaigakushi no issetsu*, pp. 283–91.

7. The Association itself, however, was torn by factional dissension as Marxian theory became fashionable in academic circles after the First World War. The series of annual national conferences on current social problems came to an end in 1924. Sumiya Etsuji, *Nihon keizaigakushi no issetsu*, p. 181.

8. See, for example, the article by Nagai Toru, "Shakai Seisaku no gempon shisō," in *Shakai Seisaku Jihō*, no. 10 (June 1921), pp. 1–21.

9. Nagai Toru, "Eikoku shihonka no sangyō heiwa ron," in *Shakai Seisaku Jihō*, no. 24 (August 1924), p. 16.

10. *Ibid.*, "Kyōchōkai shugi no dōtokuteki kiso," *Shakai Seisaku Jihō*, no. 9 (May 1921), pp. 1, 3, 4; see also Takau Shōzo, "Rōdō kaikyū ni okeru rikoshugi no hattatsu," *Shakai Seisaku Jihō* no. 7 (March 1921), pp. 176–82.

11. Nagai Toru, "Shakai Seisaku no genpon shisō," p. 7.

12. Rōmu Kondankai, p. 29.

13. From the October 1924 issue of *Asia*; quoted in Russell, p. 278.

14. *Japan Financial and Economic Monthly*, XIII, no. 10 (October 1919), p. 25.

15. Quoted from remarks made in 1928, in Ko Dan Danshaku Denki Hensan Iinkai, II, 43.

16. Quoted in Nishijima, p. 41.

17. Quoted in Yamazaki, p. 246.

18. There are, however, striking parallels between Japanese business ideology and the new emphasis on "industrial partnership" that developed in the American managerial idology of the 1920's as the classic Anglo-American ideology was modified; see Bendix, *Work and Authority*, pp. 281–308.

19. Onishi, *Asabuki Eiji kun den*, appendix, p. 68.

20. See Hirschman, p. 17. There were, however, exceptions to this generalization, particularly among Meiji entrepreneurs: see Hirschmeier's description of Nakamigawa Hikojirō and Iwasaki Yataro in *The Origins of Entrepreneurship*, pp. 218–26.

21. Reprinted in Ko Dan Danshaku Denki Hensan Iinkai, II, appendix, 152. *"Tenshoku"* is a Confucian term that had connotations similar to those of the term "calling" in Western Christianity; see Bellah, *Tokugawa Religion*, pp. 115–16. See also Onishi, *Asabuki Eiji*, appendix, p. 49.

22. "Risshin shusse o nozomu seinen ni atauru gaki," *Tōyō Keizai Shimpō*, January 15, 1928; reprinted in Ko Dan Danshaku Denki Hensan Iinkai, appendix, 96–97. *"Muga,"* here translated as "selflessness," is a Buddhist concept that might be more literally rendered as "ego-less" or "non-ego."

23. Quoted from a speech made in December 1934 to the Hamamatsu Industrial Society, in Morita Yoshio, *Keieisha dantai*, pp. 190–91.

24. Gō Seinosuke's statement in Ko Dan Danshaku Denki Hensan Iinkai, I, 1–2.

25. Makino Motojirō, *Taiken zaigo*, p. 218.

26. Kawai Tetsuo, pp. 565–68; see also the letter Hirao sent to Iwasaki Yanosuke in 1916, pp. 266–67.

27. Ko Dan Danshaku Denki Hensan Iinkai, I, 2.

28. Quoted from Mutō's report on the 1919 I.L.O. Conference in Morita Yoshio, p. 144.

29. Quoted from the *Tokyo Asahi Shimbun,* February 10, 1932, in Maruyama, p. 45.

30. See Ikeda, *Zaikai kaiko,* pp. 157–58, 173–74.

31. For accounts of these events, and the ideology of the right-wing movement, see Scalapino, *Democracy,* pp. 346–92; Delmar M. Brown; Richard Storry; Maruyama; Morris; and Byas.

32. Quoted from an English translation of the Army publication *Armies of Japan and Foreign Powers* in Cohen, p. 10. Cohen has given a detailed treatment of the development of governmental controls in the 1930's. See also Bisson, *Japan's War Economy,* pp. 13–71; Allen; and Fahs.

33. Speech reprinted in Danshaku Dan Takuma Denki Kōkankai, *Danshaku Dan,* pp. 65–71.

34. Quoted in Usami, p. 171.

35. Quoted in Yamazaki, *Kuhara Fusanosuke,* p. 39.

36. *Ibid.,* p. 227.

37. Nishijima Kyōzō, *Jigyō ō Tsuda Shingo,* p. 41.

38. Quoted in Horikoshi, p. 284.

39. "Statement of Views Regarding the New Economic Structure," issued jointly by the Japan Industrial Club, the Japanese Economic Federation, The National Federation of Industrial Organizations, and four other national groups; reprinted in Nakamura Mototada, II, 1021–26.

40. Hattori and Irimajiri, II, 182ff; Ikeda, pp. 187–89. See also the 1934 article by Mutō Sanji on the need for corporations to devote more attention and money to charitable activities: *Mutō Sanji zenshū,* I, 228–34. There is an account in English of Mitsui's efforts to create a more favorable public image in Russell, pp. 291ff.

41. Nakamura Mototada, II, 1021.

42. From the memorandum presented by Gō Seinosuke at the December 4, 1940 meeting of representatives of national business organizations; reprinted in Nakamura Mototada, II, 1011.

43. Cohen, pp. 31–33, 58–85.

44. Hirschman, p. 12.

Chapter 7

1. Sutton *et al.,* p. 366.

2. See Prothro, p. 23ff.

3. Scalapino, *Democracy,* especially pp. 246–93; see also the brief but incisive treatment of intellectual trends in the late Meiji and Taisho periods by Albert Craig in Fairbank *et al.,* pp. 529ff.

4. Scalapino, *Democracy,* p. 272.

Bibliography

Abegglen, James C. The Japanese Factory: Aspects of Its Social Organization. Glencoe, Ill.: Free Press, 1958.

Allen, G. C. Japanese Industry: Its Recent Development and Present Condition. New York: Institute of Pacific Relations, 1940.

—— A Short Economic History of Modern Japan, 1867–1937. London: George Allen & Unwin, 1946.

Arnold, Thurman. The Folklore of Capitalism. New Haven: Yale University Press, 1937.

Asano Taijirō and Asano Ryōzō. Asano Sōichirō (Asano Sōichirō). Tokyo: Aishinsha, 1923.

Ausubel, Herman. The Late Victorians. New York: D. Van Nostrand, 1955.

Ayusawa, Iwao F. Industrial Conditions and Labor Legislation in Japan. Studies and Reports, Series B, no. 16. Geneva: International Labour Office, 1926.

Ballon, Robert J. "Labor Relations in Postwar Japan: An Essay at Interpretation." Bulletin No. 9, Sophia University Socioeconomic Institute, Industrial Relations Section. Tokyo, 1966.

Beard, Miriam. A History of the Business Man. New York: Macmillan, 1938.

Bellah, Robert N. "Japan's Cultural Identity: Some Reflections on the Work of Watsuji Tetsujirō," Journal of Asian Studies, XXIV, 4 (August 1965), 573–94.

—— Tokugawa Religion: The Values of Pre-Industrial Japan. Glencoe, Ill.: Free Press, 1957.

———— "Values and Social Change in Modern Japan," in Asian Cultural Studies No. 3: Studies on Modernization of Japan by Western Scholars (Tokyo: International Christian University, 1962), 13–56.

Bendix, Reinhard. "Industrialization, Ideologies, and Social Structure," *American Sociological Review*, XXIV, 5 (October 1959), 613–23.

———— Nation-Building and Citizenship: Studies in Our Changing Social Order. New York: John Wiley & Sons, 1964.

———— "A Study of Managerial Ideologies," *Economic Development and Cultural Change*, V, 2 (January 1957), 118–28.

———— Work and Authority in Industry: Ideologies of Management in the Course of Industrialization. New York: John Wiley & Sons, 1956.

Bennett, John W., and Iwao Ishino. Paternalism in the Japanese Economy: Anthropological Studies of Oyabun-Kobun Patterns. Minneapolis: University of Minnesota Press, 1963.

Bisson, T. A. Japan's War Economy. New York: Institute of Pacific Relations, 1945.

———— Zaibatsu Dissolution in Japan. Berkeley, Calif.: University of California Press, 1954.

Blacker, Carmen. The Japanese Enlightenment: A Study of the Writings of Fukuzawa Yukichi. Cambridge, Eng.: Cambridge University Press, 1964.

Borton, Hugh. Japan Since 1931: Its Political and Social Development. New York: Institute of Pacific Relations, 1940.

Bowen, Howard R. Social Responsibilities of the Businessman. New York: Harper & Bros., 1953.

Brady, Robert A. Business as a System of Power. New York: Columbia University, 1943.

Braibanti, Ralph, and Joseph J. Spengler, Jr., eds. Tradition, Values, and Socio-Economic Development. Durham, N. C.: Duke University Press, 1961.

Brown, Delmar M. Nationalism in Japan: An Introductory Historical Analysis. Berkeley, Calif.: University of California Press, 1955.

Brown, Sidney Devere. "Okubo Toshimichi: His Political and Economic Policies in Early Meiji Japan," *Journal of Asian Studies*, XXI, 2 (February 1962), 183–97.

Burks, Ardath W. "Economics in Japanese Thought." Washington D.C.: School of Advanced International Studies, 1948. Unpublished doctoral dissertation.

Byas, Hugh. Government by Assassination. New York: Alfred A. Knopf, 1942.

Chō Yukio, ed. Jitsugyō no shisō (Business Thought). Tokyo: Chikuma Shobō, 1964.

Choi, Kee-il. "Tokugawa Feudalism and the Emergence of the New Leaders of Early Modern Japan," *Explorations in Entrepreneurial History*, IX, 2 (December 1956), 72–90.

Chūgai Shōgyō Shimpōsha, eds. Zaikai sugoroku—sensenjō no jitsugyōka (Backgammon in the Financial World: Businessmen on the Battle Line). Tokyo: Chūgai Shōgyō Shimpōsha, 1919.

Cochrane, Thomas C. The American Business System: A Historical Perspective, 1900–1955. Cambridge, Mass.: Harvard University Press, 1957.

———— Basic History of American Business. Princeton: D. Van Nostrand Co., 1959.

———— "Cultural Factors in Economic Growth," *The Journal of Economic History*, XX, 4 (December 1960), 513–30.

———— Railroad Leaders, 1845–1890: The Business Mind in Action. Cambridge, Mass.: Harvard University Press, 1953.

———— and Warren Miller. The Age of Enterprise: A Social History of Industrial America. New York: Macmillan, 1942.

Cohen, Jerome B. Japan's Economy in War and Reconstruction. Minneapolis: University of Minnesota Press, 1949.

Cole, Arthur H. Business Enterprise in Its Social Setting. Cambridge, Mass.: Harvard University Press, 1959.

———— The Historical Development of Economic and Business Literature. Boston: Baker Library, Harvard Graduate School of Business Administration, 1957.

Dahl, Robert A., Mason Haire, and Paul F. Lazerfield. Social Science Research on Business: Product and Potential. New York: Columbia University Press, 1959.

Dahrendorf, Ralf. Class and Class Conflict in Industrial Society. Stanford, Calif.: Stanford University Press, 1959.

Dai Nippon Teikoku Gikai shi (The Records of the Imperial Japanese Diet). 18 vols. Tokyo: Dai Nippon Teikoku Gikai Kankōkai, 1926–1930.

Danhof, Clarence H. "Economic Values in Cultural Perspective," in A. Dudley Ward, ed., Goals of Economic Life (New York, Harper & Bros., 1953), 84–117.

Danshaku Dan Takuma Denki Kōkankai, eds. Danshaku Dan o kataru (Talks about Baron Dan Takuma). Tokyo: Asahi Shobō, 1932.

Diamond, Sigmund. The Reputation of the American Businessman. Cambridge, Mass.: Harvard University Press, 1955.

Dore, Ronald P. "Agricultural Improvement in Japan, 1870–1900,"

Economic Development and Cultural Change, IX, 1, Part II (October 1960), 69–91.

———— City Life in Japan: A Study of a Tokyo Ward. Berkeley, Calif.: University of California Press, 1958.

———— Education in Tokugawa Japan. Berkeley, Calif.: University of California Press, 1965.

———— Land Reform in Japan. London: Oxford University Press, 1959.

Eells, Richard, and Clarence Walton. Conceptual Foundations of Business: An Outline of the Major Ideas Sustaining Business Enterprise in the Western World. Homewood, Ill.: Richard D. Irwin, 1961.

Fahs, Charles B. Government in Japan: Recent Trends in Its Scope and Operation. New York: Institute of Pacific Relations, 1940.

Fairbank, John K., Edwin O. Reischauer, and Albert M. Craig. East Asia: The Modern Transformation. Boston: Houghton Mifflin, 1965.

Fine, Sidney. Laissez Faire and the General-Welfare State: A Study of Conflict in American Thought, 1865–1901. Ann Arbor: University of Michigan Press, 1956.

Flubacher, Joseph F. The Concept of Ethics in the History of Economics. New York: Vantage Press, 1962.

Fujimoto Mitsushiro, ed. Matsukata, Kaneko monogatari (The Story of Matsukata Kojirō and Kaneko Naokichi). Kyoto: Hyōgo Shimbunsha, 1960.

Fujiwara Ginjirō. Jitsugyōjin no kimochi (The Feelings of a Businessman). Tokyo: Jitsugyō no Nihonsha, 1940.

———— The Spirit of Japanese Industry. Tokyo: Hokkuseido Press, 1940.

Fujiyama Aiichirō. Shachō gurashi sanjūnenshi (Thirty Years of Life as a Company President). Tokyo: Gakufū Shoin, 1952.

Fujiyama Raita. Atami kandanroku (Conversations at Atami). Tokyo: Chūō Kōronsha, 1938.

Fukuzawa Momosuke. Seiyō bummei no botsuroku, tōyō bummei no bokkō (The Decline of Western Civilization and the Rise of Eastern Civilization). Tokyo: Daiyamondosha, 1932.

Fukuzawa Yukichi. Fukuō hyakuwa (A Hundred Discourses by Fukuzawa Yukichi). Kadogawa Shoten: 1954.

———— Fukuzawa zenshū (The Collected Works of Fukuzawa), edited by Jiji Shimpōsha. 10 vols. Tokyo: Kokumin Tosho K.K., 1926.

———— Zoku Fukuzawa zenshū (The Collected Works of Fukuzawa, Continued), edited by Keio Gijuku. 7 vols. Tokyo: Iwanami Shoten, 1933.

Furusada Yoshimasa, ed. Kōkoku ronshū oyobi jimbutsu hyōden (Critical Biographies and Selected Talks on Making the Country Prosper). Tokyo: Kōkoku no Nihonsha, 1913.

Gerschenkron, Alexander. Economic Backwardness in Historical Perspective: A Book of Essays. Cambridge, Mass.: Harvard University Press, 1962.

Girvetz, Harry K. The Evolution of Liberalism. New York: Collier Books, 1963.

Glover, J. D. The Attack on Big Business. Boston: Harvard Graduate School of Business Administration, 1954.

Godai Ryūsaku, ed. Godai Tomoatsu den (A Biography of Godai Tomoatsu). Tokyo: Godai Ryūsaku, 1933.

Gō Danshaku Kinenkai, eds. Danshaku Gō Seinosuke kun den (A Biography of Baron Gō Seinosuke). Tokyo: Gō Danshaku Kinenkai, 1943.

Gras, N. S. B. Business and Capitalism: An Introduction to Business History. New York: F. S. Crofts, 1939.

Hall, Robert King. Shūshin: The Ethics of a Defeated Nation. New York: Bureau of Publications, Teachers College, Columbia University, 1949.

Hara Kunizō, ed. Hara Rokurō den (A Biography of Hara Rokurō). Tokyo: Hara Kunizō, 1937.

Hartmann, Heinz. Authority and Organization in German Management. Princeton: Princeton University Press, 1959.

Hartz, Louis. Economic Policy and Democratic Thought: Pennsylvania, 1776–1860. Cambridge, Mass.: Harvard University Press, 1948.

Hashimoto Keizaburō. Waga kaikokuroku (My Memoirs). Tokyo: Sekiyū Bunkasha, 1958.

Hattori Shisō and Irimajiri Yoshinaga, eds. Kindai Nihon jimbutsu keizaishi (A Biographic Economic History of Modern Japan). 2 vols. Tokyo: Tōyō Keizai Shimpōsha, 1955.

Hazama Hiroshi. Nihon rōmu kanrishi kenkyū—keiei kazokushugi no keisei to hatten (Studies in the History of Labor Management in Japan: The Establishment and Development of Administrative Familism). Tokyo: Daiyamondosha, 1964.

Hirschman, Albert O. The Strategy of Economic Development. New Haven and London: Yale University Press, 1961. Paperbound edition.

Hirschmeier, Johannes. The Origins of Entrepreneurship in Meiji Japan. Cambridge, Mass.: Harvard University Press, 1964.

———— "Keizai hatten no tame no kigyōka kyōkyū" ("The Supply of Entrepreneurs for Economic Development"), *Akademia,* 32 (December 1961), 25–48.

———— "Shibusawa Eiichi: Industrial Pioneer," in William W. Lockwood, ed., The State and Economic Enterprise in Japan (Princeton: Princeton University Press, 1965), 209–47.

Hōchi Shimbun Keizaibu, eds. Zaikai hizakurige (Around the World of Finance on Shanks' Mare). Tokyo: Tōyō Keizai Shimpōsha, 1928.

Hofstadter, Richard. Social Darwinism in American Thought: 1860–1915. Philadelphia: University of Pennsylvania Press, 1945.

Honjō Eijirō. Economic Theory and History of Japan in the Tokugawa Period. Tokyo: Maruzen Co., 1943.

———— Kinsei no keizai shisō (Early Modern Economic Thought). Tokyo: Hyōronsha, 1933.

———— Kinsei no keizai shisō—zokuhen (Early Modern Economic Thought, Continued). Tokyo: Hyōronsha, 1938.

———— Nihon keizai shisōshi (A History of Japanese Economic Thought). Tokyo: Yūhikaku, 1958.

Horie, Yasuzō. "Business Pioneers of Modern Japan: Ishikawa Masatatsu and Oshima Takato," *Kyoto University Economic Review,* XXX, 2 (October 1960), 1–16.

———— "Modern Entrepreneurship in Meiji Japan," in William W. Lookwood, ed., The State and Economic Enterprise in Japan (Princeton: Princeton University Press, 1965), 183–208.

Horikoshi Teizō, ed. Keizai Dantai Rengōkai zenshi (The Federation of Economic Organizations: Early History). Tokyo: Keizai Dantai Rengōkai, 1962.

Hoselitz, Bert F. The Progress of Underdeveloped Areas. Chicago: University of Chicago Press, 1952.

Ienaga Saburō, Gairai bunka sesshu shiron—kindai seiyō bunka sesshu no shisōteki kōsatsu (A History of the Adoption of Foreign Culture: An Inquiry into the Intellectual History of the Adoption of Modern Western Culture). Tokyo: Iwanami Shoten, 1948.

———— Nihon no dōtoku shisōshi (A History of Japanese Ethics). Tokyo: Iwanami Shoten, 1954.

————— *et al.,* eds. Iwanami kōza Nihon no rekishi (Iwanami History of Japan), Vol. XVIII. Tokyo: Iwanami Shoten, 1963.

Ienaka Shigeru. Ikeo Yoshizō o kataru (A Discussion of Ikeo Yoshizō). Tokyo: Fujii Shoten, 1939.

Ike, Nobutaka. The Beginnings of Political Democracy in Japan. Baltimore: Johns Hopkins Press, 1950.

Ikeda Seihin. Kojin konjin (Men of the Past and Present). Tokyo: Sekai no Nihonsha, 1949.

——— Watakushi no ningenkan (My View of Life). Tokyo: Bungei Shunjūsha, 1951.

——— Zaikai kaiko (Recollections of the Financial World). Tokyo: Sekai no Nihonsha, 1949.

Imai Gosuke Ō Denki Kankō Iinkai, eds. Imai Gosuke ō den (A Biography of Imai Gosuke). Tokyo: Nishigahara Dōzōkai, 1959.

Inoue Kaoru Kō Denki Hensankai, eds. Seigai Inoue kō den (A Biography of Prince Inoue Seigai Kaoru). 5 vols. Tokyo: Naigai Shoseki, 1933–34.

International Labour Office, Industrial Labour in Japan (Geneva: International Labour Office, 1933), Studies and Reports, Series A, No. 37.

Irimajiri Yoshinaga. Iwasaki Yatarō (Iwasaki Yatarō). Tokyo: Yoshikawa Kōbundō, 1960.

——— ed. Kōchi Shōkō Kaigisho shichijūnenshi (Seventy Years of the Kochi Chamber of Commerce and Industry). Kochi: Kōchi Shōkō Kaigisho, 1961.

Ishiyama Kenkichi. Makino Motojirō kun o kataru (A Discussion of Makino Motojirō). Tokyo: Gakugei, 1937.

Itō Hirobumi. Hisho ruisan (Classified Collection of Confidential Papers). 25 vols. Tokyo: Hisho Ruisan Kankōkai, 1933–36.

Itō Toshio, ed. Ōsaka Shōkō Kaigisho shichijūgonenshi (Seventy-five Years of the Osaka Chamber of Commerce and Industry). Osaka: Ōsaka Shōkō Kaigisho, 1955.

Itō Yoshio *et al.*, eds. Kindai Nihon shisōshi kōza (Series on Modern Japanese Intellectual History), Vol. V. Tokyo: Chikuma Shobō, 1960.

Itsukakai, eds. Furukawa Ichibe ō den (A Biography of Furukawa Ichibe). Tokyo: Itsukakai, 1926.

Iwasaki Seishichi, Zaikai gakuya manda (Random Talk from Behind the Scenes of the Financial World). Tokyo: Fusan Shobō, 1939.

Iwata Masakazu, Okubo Toshimichi: The Bismarck of Japan. Berkeley, Calif.: University of California Press, 1965.

Jansen, Marius B., ed. Changing Japanese Attitudes toward Modernization. Princeton: Princeton University Press, 1965.

——— Sakamoto Ryōma and the Meiji Restoration. Princeton: Princeton University Press, 1961.

Japan Financial and Economic Monthly. Tokyo: 1919–22.

Jenks, Leland H. "Business Ideology," *Explorations in Entrepreneurial History*, X, 1 (October 1957), 1–7.

Jiji Tsūshinsha Henshūkyoku, eds. Daihyōteki jimbutsu oyobi jigyō (Exemplary Personalities and Enterprises). Tokyo: Jiji Tsūshinsha, 1913.

Jitsugyō no Nihon (Business Japan). Tokyo: 1897–1919.

Jitsugyō no Sekaisha Henshūkyoku, eds. Mitsui to Mitsubishi (Mitsui and Mitsubishi). Tokyo: Jitsugyō no Sekaisha, 1913.

Kada Tetsuji. Meiji shoki shakai keizai shisōshi (A History of Social and Economic Thought in Early Meiji). Tokyo: Iwanami Shoten, 1937.

Kajinishi Mitsuhaya. Sangyō shi no hitobito (Men in the History of Industry). Tokyo: Tōkyō Daigaku Shuppankai, 1954.

Kakuyūkai, eds. Okura Kakugen ō (Okura Kihachirō). Tokyo: Minyūsha, 1924.

Kanazawa, Yoshio. "The Regulation of Corporate Enterprise: The Law of Unfair Competition and the Control of Monopoly Power," in Arthur Taylor von Mehren, ed., Law in Japan: The Legal Order in a Changing Society (Cambridge, Mass.: Harvard University Press, 1963), 480–506.

Kanda Kōichi. Nihon kōjōhō to rōdō hogo (The Factory Law and the Protection of Labor in Japan). Tokyo: Dōbunkan, 1919.

Kataoka Naoharu. Kaisō roku (Memoirs). Kyoto: Hyakkoya Bunko, 1932.

Kawai Eijirō. Meiji shisōshi no ichi dammen—Kanai Noboru o chūshin to shite (One Aspect of Meiji Intellectual History: Kanai Noboru). Tokyo: Nihon Hyōronsha, 1941.

Kawai Tetsuo. Hirao Hachisaburō (Hirao Hachisaburō). Tokyo: Hanada Shobō, 1952.

Kawashima Takeyoshi. Ideorogii to shite no kazoku seidō (The Family System as Ideology). Tokyo: Iwanami Shoten, 1957.

Kazahaya Yasoji. Nihon shakai seisakushi (The History of Social Policies in Japan). 2d ed. Tokyo: Nihon Hyōronsha, 1947.

Kerr, Clark, John T. Dunlap, Frederick H. Harbison, and Charles A. Meyers. Industrialism and Industrial Man: The Problems of Labor and Management in Economic Growth. 2d ed. New York: Oxford University Press, 1964.

Key, V. O., Jr. Politics, Parties, and Pressure Groups. 5th ed. New York: Thomas Y. Crowell, 1964.

Kirkland, Edward Chase. Dream and Thought in the Business Community, 1860–1900. Ithaca, N.Y.: Cornell University Press, 1956.

Kishimoto Eitarō. Nihon zettaishugi no shakai seisakushi (A History of the Social Policies of Japanese Absolutism). Tokyo: Yūhikaku, 1955.

Kitabayashi Sōkichi. Asano Sōichirō den (A Biography of Asano Sōichirō). Tokyo: Chikura Shobō, 1930.
Ko Dan Danshaku Denki Hensan Iinkai, eds. Danshaku Dan Takuma den (A Biography of Baron Dan Takuma). 2 vols. Tokyo: Ko Dan Danshaku Denki Hensan Iinkai, 1938.
Kobayashi Ichizō. Jihen wa dō katazuka ka (How Can the Emergency Be Brought to an End?). Tokyo: Jitsugyō no Nihonsha, 1939.
Kosaka Masaki, ed. Japanese Thought in the Meiji Era. Tokyo: The Centenary Culture Council, 1958.
——— "The World and Meiji Japan," *Philosophical Studies of Japan*, VIII (1961), 57–77.
Kuwada Ichizō. Kōjōhō to rōdō hoken (The Factory Law and Labor Insurance). Tokyo: Ryūbunkan, 1909.
——— Shakai seisaku (Social Policy). Tokyo: Waseda Daigaku Shuppanbun, 1908.
Kuznets, Simon S., Wilbert E. Moore, and Joseph J. Spengler, eds. Economic growth: Brazil, India, Japan. Durham, N.C.: Duke University Press, 1955.
Kyōchōkai, eds. Kyōchōkai jigyō ippan (An Outline of the Activities of the Kyōchōkai). Tokyo: Kyōchōkai, 1923.
——— eds. Saikin no shakai undō (Social Movements in Recent Times). Tokyo: Kyōchōkai, 1929.
Laski, Harold J. The Rise of European Liberalism: An Essay in Interpretation. 2d ed. London: Unwin Books, 1962.
Levenson, Joseph. " 'History' and 'Value': the Tensions of Intellectual Choice in Modern China," in Arthur Wright, ed., Studies in Chinese Thought. Chicago: University of Chicago Press, 1953.
Levine, Solomon B. Industrial Relations in Postwar Japan. Urbana: University of Illinois Press, 1958.
——— "Labor Markets and Collective Bargaining in Japan," in William W. Lockwood, ed., The State and Economic Enterprise in Japan (Princeton: Princeton University Press, 1965), 633–67.
Lockwood, William W. The Economic Development of Japan: Growth and Structural Change, 1868–1938. Princeton: Princeton University Press, 1954.
——— "Economic and Political Modernization: Japan," in Robert E. Ward and Dankwart A. Rustow, eds., Political Modernization in Japan and Turkey (Princeton: Princeton University Press, 1964), 117–45.
——— "The Political Consequences of Economic Development in Japan." A paper prepared for the Japanese Studies Seminar, May 1962, at International House, Tokyo, mimeographed.

————, ed. The State and Economic Enterprise in Japan. Princeton, N.J.: Princeton University Press, 1965.

Maeda Masana, "Kōgyō iken" ("Views on Promoting Industry"). Reprinted in Ouchi Hyoei and Tsuchiya Takao, eds. Meiji zenki zaisei keizai shiryō shūsei (Collection of Historical Materials on Finance and Economy of the Early Meiji Period). Vol. XVIII. Tokyo, Kaizosha, 1931–36.

McClosky, Robert G. American Conservatism in the Age of Enterprise: A Study of William Graham Sumner, Stephen J. Field and Andrew Carnegie. Cambridge, Mass.: Harvard University Press, 1951.

McEwan, J. R. The Political Writings of Ogyū Sorai. Cambridge, Eng.: Cambridge University Press, 1962.

McGuire, Joseph W. Business and Society. New York: McGraw-Hill, 1963.

McLaren, W. W., ed. "Japanese Government Documents," *Transactions of the Asiatic Society of Japan*, XLII, Part 1. Tokyo, 1914.

Makino Motojirō. Watakushi no shoseihō—yo ni sho suru kokorogamae (My Rules for Success: Preparation for Getting Along in the World). Tokyo: Konnichi no Mondaisha, 1937.

————— Taiken zaigo (Talks on My Experiences in Finance). Tokyo: Jitsugyō no Nihonsha, 1939.

Makino Ryōzō. Nakahashi Tokugorō (Nakahashi Tokugorō), 2 vols. Tokyo: Nakahashi Tokugorō Ō Denki Hensankai, 1944.

Marris, Robin. The Economic Theory of 'Managerial' Capitalism. New York: The Free Press of Glencoe, 1964.

Maruyama Masao. Thought and Behavior in Modern Japanese Politics. London: Oxford University Press, 1963.

Masuda Harukichi. Senji keizai o suishin suru hitobito (The Men behind the Wartime Economy). Tokyo: Shinkigensha, 1941.

Masuda Takashi, Jijo Masuda Takashi ō den (The Autobiography of Masuda Takashi). Tokyo: Uchida Kōkaku Ho, 1939.

Matsumoto Kenjirō. Kaikyūdan (Reminiscences). Tokyo: Masu Shobō, 1952.

————— Okashikeriya warae (Laugh If It Is Amusing). Tokyo: Tenbōsha, 1959.

Matsunaga Yasuzaemon. Tantan roku (Chats). Tokyo: Keizai Oraisha, 1950.

Matsushita Denkichi. Zaibatsu Mitsui no shin kenkyū (A New Study of the Mitsui Zaibatsu). Tokyo: Chūgai Sangyō Chōsa, 1936.

Meiji bunka shiryō sōsho (Collected Documents on Meiji Culture). Obama Toshie, ed. 2 vols. Tokyo: Kazama Shobō, 1961.

Meiji bunka zenshū (Collected Works on Meiji Culture). Yoshino Sakuzō, ed. 24 vols. Tokyo: Nihon Hyōronsha, 1928–30.

Meiji bunka zenshū, XV, zoku shakai hen (Collected Works on Meiji Culture: Supplement to the Volume on Society). Vol. XV. Tokyo: Meiji Bunka Kenkyukai, 1957. Revised edition.

Miller, William, ed. Men in Business: Essays in the History of Entrepreneurship. Cambridge, Mass.: Harvard University Press, 1952.

Mitsuoka Takeo, ed. Yuri Kimimasa den (A Biography of Yuri Kimimasa). Tokyo: Kōyūkan, 1916.

Miyamoto Mataji. Kabunakama no kenkyū (Studies on Guilds). Tokyo: Yūhikaku, 1938.

———— Nihon girudo no kaiho—Meiji ishin to kabu nakama (The Breakup of Guilds in Japan: The Meiji Restoration and kabu nakama). Tokyo: Yūhikaku, 1957.

———— Osaka chōnin (Osaka Townsmen). Tokyo: Kōbundō, 1957.

———— Osaka jimbutsu shi—Osaka o kizuita hitobito (A History of the Men of Osaka: The Men who Built Osaka). Tokyo: Kōbundō, 1960.

———— Osaka shōnin (Osaka Merchants). Tokyo: Kōbundō, 1958.

Monsen, Joseph R., Jr. Modern American Capitalism: Ideologies and Issues. Boston: Houghton Mifflin, 1963.

Moore, Wilbert E. "The Social Framework of Economic Development," in Ralph Braibanti and Joseph J. Spengler, eds., Tradition, Values, and Socio-Economic Development (Durham, N.C.: Duke University Press, 1961), 57–82.

Morita Muteki. Yano Tsuneta to Daiichi Seimei (Yano Tsuneta and the Daiichi Life Insurance Company). Tokyo: Nihon Hyōronsha, 1938.

Morita Yoshio. Nihon keieisha dantai hatten shi (A History of the Development of Management Organizations in Japan). Tokyo: Nikkan Rōdō Tsūshinsha, 1958.

Morris, Ivan, ed. Japan, 1931–1945. Boston: D. C. Heath, 1963.

Motegi Gentarō. Otani Kahyōe ō den (A Biography of Otani Kahyōe). Yokohama: Otani Kahyōe O Shōtokukai, 1931.

Mutō Sanji. Mutō Sanji Zenshū Kankōkai, ed. Mutō Sanji zenshū (The Collected Works of Mutō Sanji). Vol. I. Tokyo: Shingisha, 1963.

Nagai Michio. "Herbert Spencer in Early Meiji Japan," *Far Eastern Quarterly*, XIV, 1 (November 1954), 55–64.

Nagai Toru. "Shakai Seisaku no gempon shiso" ("The Basic Ideas of Social Policy") in *Shakai Seisaku Jihō*, (June 1921), 1–21.

———— "Kyōchōkai shugi no dōtokutei kiso" ("The Moral Basis of the Principle of Kyōchō"), in *Shakai Seisaku Jihō*, IX (May 1921), 1.

———— "Eikoku shihonka no sangyō heiwa ron" ("The Arguments of British Capitalists for Industrial Peace"), in *Shakai Seisaku Jihō*, XXIV (August 1924), 16.

Nagata Masaomi. "Nihon shihonka dantai shōshi" ("A Short History of Capitalist Organizations in Japan"), *Keizai Hyōron*, III, 8, 9, 10 (August, September, October 1954), 140–50, 85–95, 110–20.

Nagoya Shōkō Kaigisho, eds. Nagoya Shōkō Kaigisho gojūnenshi (Fifty Years of the Nagoya Chamber of Commerce and Industry). Nagoya: Nagoya Shōkō Kaigisho, 1941.

Nakagawa Keiichiro, "Organized Entrepreneurship in the Course of Industrialization of Prewar Japan." Paper read before the International Conference on Economic Growth at Tokyo. September 1966. Mimeographed.

Nakajima Kumakichi. Seikai zaikai gojūnen (Fifty Years in the Worlds of Politics and Finance). Tokyo: Dai Nihon Yuban Kōdansha, 1951.

Nakamura Katsunori. "Suzuki Bunji to Taishō rōdō undō" ("Suzuki Bunji and the Labor Movement in the Taishō Period"), *Hōgaku Kenkyū*, XXXII, 1, 2–3, 6 (January, February, June 1959), 43–67, 139–63, 481–510.

Nakamura Mototada, ed. Nihon Kōgyō Kurabu nijūgonenshi (Twenty-five Years of the Japan Industrial Club). 2 vols. Tokyo: Nihon Kōgyō Kurabu, 1943.

Nakarai Tōsui, ed. Doi Michio kun den (A Biography of Doi Michio). Tokyo: Nonaka Masao, 1924.

Nakase Toshikazu. "Kensei yōgo shisō no shinshutsu to tenkai—daiichi goken undō no shidō riron" ("The Birth and Development of the Idea of Defending the Constitution: Leading Theories in the First goken undō"), *Shigaku Zasshi*, LXXII, 2 (February 1963), 48–79.

Nihō Sensei Shōden Hensankai, eds. Yamamoto Nihō sensei shōden (A Short Biography of Yamamoto Teijirō). Tokyo: Nihō Sensei Shōden Hensankai, 1941.

Nihon kindaishi jiten (A Dictionary of Modern Japanese History). Kyōtō Daigaku Bungakubu Kokushikenkyūshitsu and Nihon Kindaishi Jiten Henshū Iinkai, eds. Tokyo: Tōyō Keizai Shimpōsha, 1958.

Nihon rōdō undō shiryō (Documents on the History of Japanese Labor Movements). 11 vols. Tokyo: Rōdō Undō Shiryō Iinkai, 1962.

Nishihara Yūjirō, ed. Fujiyama Raita den (A Biography of Fujiyama Raita). Tokyo: Fujiyama Aiichirō, 1939.

Nishijima Kyōzō. Jigyō ō Tsuda Shingo (Tsuda Shingo: King of Enterprise). Tokyo: Konnichi no Mondai, 1938.

Nishikawa Shōjirō. Yū ō (Iba Teigo), n.p., 1931. Reprinted 1952.

Noda Kazuo, "Meiji no kigyō seishin" ("The Spirit of the Meiji Entrepreneur"), *Bessatsu Chūō Kōron*, II, 1 (Summer 1963), 213–26.

———— Nihon no jūyaku (Big Business Executives in Japan). Tokyo: Daimondosha, 1960.

Okubo Toshimichi monjo (The Papers of Okubo Toshimichi) 10 vols. Tokyo, Nihon Shiseki Kyōkai, 1927–29.

Nomura Kentarō. Gaikan Nihon keizai shisōshi (A Survey History of Japanese Economic Thought). Tokyo: Keio Shuppansha, 1949. Revised edition.

———— "Fukuzawa Yukichi no keizairon" ("The Economic Theories of Fukuzawa Yukichi"), *Tōyō Keizai Shimpō*, 2288, 2289, 2290 (September 1947), 20–21, 6, 20–21.

Obata Kyugoro. An Interpretation of the Life of Viscount Shibusawa. Tokyo: The Viscount Shibusawa Memorial Foundation, 1937.

Odaka Kunio. "Traditionalism, Democracy in Japanese Industry," *Industrial Relations: A Journal of Economy and Society,* III, 1 (October 1963), 95–103.

Ogura Masatane. Ogura Masatane dansō (Talks by Ogura Masatane). Tokyo: Kōkoan, 1955.

Okano Seigō. Kane, mono, kokoro (Money, Things, and Heart). Tokyo: Zenkoku Shobō, 1941.

Okochi Kazuo. Reimeiki no Nihon rōdō undō (The Dawn of the Japanese Labor Movement). Tokyo: Iwanami Shoten, 1953.

———— Labor in Modern Japan. Tokyo: The Science Council of Japan, 1958.

Okuma monjo (The Papers of Okuma Shigenobu). 5 vols. Tokyo: Waseda Daigaku Shakaikagaku Kenkyūkai, 1959.

Okuma Shigenobu. Okuma haku shakai kan (Count Okuma's Views of Society). Tokyo: Kano Seikōkan, 1910.

———— comp. Fifty Years of New Japan, 2 vols. New York: Dutton & Co., 1909.

Olson, Lawrence. Dimensions of Japan: A Collection of Reports Written for the American Universities Field Staff. New York: American Universities Field Staff, 1963.

Omachi Kaigetsu. Hakushagu Gotō Shōjirō (A Biography of Count Gotō Shojirō). Tokyo: Fuzambō, 1914.

Onishi Rihei. Asabuki Eiji kun den (A Biography of Asabuki Eiji). Tokyo: Asabuki Eiji Denki Hensankai, 1928.
—— ed. Fukuzawa Momosuke ō den (A Biography of Fukuzawa Momosuke). Tokyo: Fukuzawa Momosuke O Denki Hensanjo, 1939.
Ozaki Shōichi. Sankai ijin Otani Kōzō (Otani Kōzō: A Great Man in the World of Silk). Saranishimura, Nagano Prefecture, Otani Kōzō O Igyō Kenshokai, 1914. 2d ed. 1951.
Palm, Franklin Charles. The Middle Class Then and Now. New York: Macmillan, 1936.
Pelzel, John. "The Small Industrialist in Japan," Explorations in Entrepreneurial History, VII, 2 (December 1954), 79–93.
Prothro, James Warren. The Dollar Decade: Business Ideas in the 1920's. Baton Rouge: Lousiana State University Press, 1954.
Ranis, Gustav. "The Community-Centered Entrepreneur in Japanese Development," Explorations in Entrepreneurial History, VIII, 2 (December 1955), 80–97.
Reishauer, Edwin O. Japan, Past and Present. 2d ed. New York: Alfred A. Knopf, 1953.
Research Center in Entrepreneurial History at Harvard University. Change and the Entrepreneur: Postulates and Patterns for Entrepreneurial History. Cambridge, Mass.: Harvard University Press, 1949.
"Rōdō kumiaihō hantai no tame sakusei shitaru shiryō, II—yori Showa gonen made Showa rokunen" ("Materials for the Formulation of Policy in Opposition to the Labor Union Bill, II: 1930–31"), Nihon Kōgyō Kurabu Chōsaka. In the files of the Japan Industrial Club.
Roggendorf, Joseph, ed. Studies in Japanese Culture: Tradition and Experiment. Tokyo: Sophia University, 1963.
Rōmu Kondankai, eds. Rōdōsha shokun! naze zenkoku jitsugyōka dantai wa rōdō kumiai hoan ni hantai shita ka ("Workers! Why have Business Groups Throughout the Country Opposed the Labor Union Bill?"), n.p., Rōdō Kondankai, n.d.
Rostow, Walter W. The Stages of Economic Growth: A Non-Communist Manifesto. Cambridge, Eng. Cambridge University Press, 1960.
Russell, Oland D. The House of Mitsui. Boston: Little, Brown, 1939.
Sakata Yoshio. "Shikon-shōsairon to shizoku shusshin jitsugyōka" ("Samurai Spirit and Commercial Talent and Businessmen of Samurai Origins"), Jinbun Gakuhō, XIX (February 1964), 1–28.
Sakurayabashi Makoto and Robert J. Ballon. "Labor-Management

Relations in Modern Japan: A Historical Survey of Personnel Administration," in Joseph Roggendorf, ed., Studies in Japanese Culture: Tradition and Experiment (Tokyo: Sophia University, 1963), 245–66.

"Sangyō iinkai hoan ni taisuru iken narabi ni sankō shiryō" ("Reference Materials and Opinions concerning the Labor Bill of the Committee on Industry"). Nihon Kōgyō Kurabu Chōsaka. May 1929. In the files of the Japan Industrial Club.

Sansom, George B. The Western World and Japan. London: The Cresset Press, 1950.

Scalapino, Robert A. Democracy and the Party Movement in Prewar Japan: The Failure of the First Attempt. Berkeley, Calif.: University of California Press, 1953.

———— "Ideology and Modernization—The Japanese Case," in David E. Apter, ed., Ideology and Discontent (New York: The Free Press of Glencoe, 1964), 93–127.

———— "Japan," in Walter Galenson, ed., Labor and Economic Development (New York: John Wiley & Sons, 1959), 75–145.

Schermerhorn, Richard A. Society and Power. New York: Random House, 1961.

Schlatter, Richard. Private Property: The History of an Idea. New Brunswick, N.J.: Rutgers University Press, 1951.

Schumpeter, E. G., ed. The Industrialization of Japan and Manchukuo, 1930–1940. New York: Macmillan, 1940.

Shakai Seisaku Gakkai, eds. Kōjōhō to rōdō mondai (The Labor Problem and Factory Legislation). Tokyo: Dōbunkan, 1908.

———— eds. Rōdō sōgi (Labor Disputes). Tokyo: Dōbunkan, 1914.

Shakai Seisaku Jihō (The Social Reform: The Journal of the Kyōchōkai). Tokyo, 1920–1921.

Sheldon, Charles David. The Rise of the Merchant Class in Tokugawa Japan, 1600–1868: An Introductory Survey. Locust Valley, N.Y.: J. J. Augustin, 1958.

Shibusawa Eiichi. Seien Hyakuwa (A Hundred Discourses by Shibusawa). 2 vols. Tokyo: Dōbunkan, 1912.

Shibusawa Eiichi denki shiryō (Biographical Materials on Shibusawa Eiichi). 50 vols. Tokyo: Shibusawa Seien Kinen Zaidan Ryūmonsha, 1955–1963. Herein cited as SEDS.

Shimada Saburō (Yoshino Sakuzō, ed.) Shimada Saburō zenshū (Collected Works of Shimada Saburō). Tokyo: Keieisha Shoten, 1924.

Shimbun shūsei Meiji hennenshi (A Chronological History of Meiji, Compiled from Newspapers). 15 vols. Nakayama Yasumasa, ed. Tokyo: Shimbun Shūsei Meiji Hennenshi Hensankai, 1935.

Shindo Takejiro. Labor in the Japanese Cotton Industry. Tokyo: Japan Society for the Promotion of Science, 1961.

Shirayanagi Shūko. Nakamigawa Hikojirō den (A Biography of Nakamigawa Hikojirō). Tokyo: Iwanami Shoten, 1940.

Shively, Donald H. "Motoda Eifu: Confucian Lecturer to the Meiji Emperor," in David S. Nivison and Arthur F. Wright, eds., Confucianism in Action (Stanford, Calif.: Stanford University Press, 1959), 303–33.

——— "Nishimura Shigeki: A Confucian View of Modernization," in Marius B. Jansen, ed., Changing Japanese Attitudes toward Modernization (Princeton: Princeton University Press, 1965), 193–241.

Shōgyō Kaigisho Rengōkai, eds. Shōgyō Kaigisho no kako oyobi genzai (The Chamber of Commerce: Past and Present). Tokyo: Shōgyō Kaigisho Rengōkai, 1924.

Shōkō Gyōseishi Kankōkai, eds. Shōkō gyōseishi (A History of Government Administration of Commerce and Industry). 3 vols. Tokyo: Shōkō Gyōseishi Kankōkai, 1955.

Shukuri Shigeichi, Shōda Heigorō (Shōda Heigorō). Tokyo: Taikyōsha, 1932.

Smith, Adam. An Inquiry into the Nature and Cause of the Wealth of Nations. New York: Modern Library, 1937.

Smith, Thomas C. The Agrarian Origins of Modern Japan. Stanford, Calif.: Stanford University Press, 1959.

——— "The Discontented," *Journal of Asian Studies*, XXI, 2 (February 1962), 215–19.

——— "Japan's Aristocratic Revolution," *Yale Review*, L (1964), 370–83.

——— "Landlords' Sons in the Business Elite," *Economic Development and Cultural Change*, IX, 1, Part II (October 1960), 93–107.

——— "Old Values and New Techniques in the Modernization of Japan," *Far Eastern Quarterly*, XIV, 3 (May 1955), 355–63.

——— Political Change and Industrial Development in Japan: Government Enterprise, 1868–1880. Stanford, Calif.: Stanford University Press, 1955.

Smith, Warren W., Jr. Confucianism in Modern Japan: A Study of Conservatism in Japanese Intellectual History. Tokyo: Hokkuseido Press, 1959.

Stead, Albert, ed. Japan by the Japanese: A Survey by Its Highest Authorities. New York: Dodd, Mead & Co., 1904.

Storry, Richard. The Double Patriots: A Study of Japanese Nationalism. Boston: Houghton Mifflin, 1957.

Sutton, Francis X., Seymour E. Harris, Carl Kaysen, and James Tobin. The American Business Creed. Cambridge, Mass.: Harvard University Press, 1956.

Sumiya Etsuji. Nihon keizaigakushi (A History of the Study of Economics in Japan). Tokyo: Mineruva Shobō, 1958.

———— Nihon keizaigakushi no issetsu—Shakai Seisaku Gakkai o chūshin to shite (One Phase of the History of the Study of Economics in Japan: The Association for the Study of Social Policy). Tokyo: Nihon Hyōronsha, 1948.

———— et al. "Shakai Seisaku Gakkai nenpu" ("A Chronology of the Association for the Study of Social Policy"), Shakai Seisaku Gakkai Nenpō, VIII (1960), 233–51.

Sumiya Mikio, "Kokuminteki vijyon no tōgō to bunkai" ("The Formulation and Breakdown of a National Vision"), Itō Yoshi et al., eds. in Kindai shisōshi kōza (Series on Modern Japanese Intellectual History). Tokyo: Chikuma Shobō, 1960, V, 9–42.

———— Nihon chinrōdō shiron—Meiji zenki ni okeru rōdō shakaikyū no keisei (A History of Wage Labor in Japan: The Formation of the Laboring Class in the Early Meiji Period). Tokyo: Tōkyō Daigaku Shuppankai, 1955.

———— "Rōdō undō ni okeru shinri to ronri" ("Psychology and Logic in the Labor Movement"), in Itō Yoshi et al., eds., Kindai Nihon shisōshi kōza. Tokyo: Chikuma Shobō, 1960, V, 187–217.

———— "Shakai undō no hassei to shakai shisō" ("Social Thought and the Birth of the Social Movement"), in Ienaga Saburō et al., eds., Iwanami kōza Nihon no Rekishi (Iwanami History of Japan). Tokyo: Iwanami Shoten, 1963, XVIII, 153–96.

Suzuki Bunji. Rōdō undō nijunen (Twenty Years in the Labor Movement). Tokyo: Ichigensha, 1931.

Suzuki Gorō. Suzuki Tōsaburō den—Nihon kindai sangyō no senku (A Biography of Suzuki Tōsaburō: Pioneer of Modern Japanese Industry). Tokyo: Tōyō Keizai Shimpō, 1956.

Swearingen, Rodger, and Paul Langer. Red Flag in Japan: International Communism in Action, 1919–1951. Cambridge, Mass.: Harvard University Press, 1952.

Takahashi Korekiyo. Zuisō roku (A Record of Random Thoughts). Tokyo: Chikura Shobō, 1936.

———— Takahashi Korekiyo Jiden (The Autobiography of Takahashi Korekiyo). Tokyo: Chikura Shobō, 1936.

Takahashi Toshitaro. Mitsui Bussan no omoide (Memories of the Mitsui Trading Company). Tokyo: Kyōbunkan, 1937.

Takase Senba. Tōkyō Shōkō Kaigisho hachijūnen no kaiko (The

Tokyo Chamber of Commerce and Industry: Eighty Years in Retrospect). Tokyo: Tōkyō Shōkō Kaigisho, 1961.

Takau Shōzō. "Rōdō kaikyu ni okeru rikoshugi no hattatsu" (The Development of Selfishness in the Working Class), in *Shakai Seisaku Jihō*, VII (March 1921), 176–82.

Takimoto Seiichi, ed. Nihon keizai sōsho (Collected Works on Japanese Economics). 36 vols. Tokyo: Nihon Keizai Sōsho Kankōkai, 1914–17.

Tamura Gyakusui. Seikō to jinkaku (Success and Character). Tokyo: Hakubunkan, 1907.

Tanaka Chūji, ed. Toyoda Sakichi den (A Biography of Toyoda Sakichi). Nagoya: Toyoda Sakichi Ō Seiden Hensanjo, 1933.

Taylor, William H., and Robert A. Brady. "Policy Centralization in Japan under the Kokutai Principle," *Pacific Affairs*, XIV, 1 (March 1941), 51–77.

"Teikoku Gikai Shūgiin giji sokkiroku" ("Stenographic Record of the Proceedings of the House of Representatives of the Imperial Diet"), in *Kampō gōkai* (Supplement to the Official Gazette), Tokyo.

Teikoku Gikai Shūgiin iinkai kaigiroku (Minutes of the Committee Proceedings of the House of Representatives of the Imperial Diet). Tokyo: Shūgiin Jimukyoku.

Tetsudō Shō, eds. Nihon tetsudō shi (A History of Japanese Railroads). 3 vols. Tokyo: Tetsudō Shō, 1921.

Tokutomi Ichirō. Kōshaku Matsukata Masayoshi den (A Biography of Prince Matsukata Masayoshi). 2 vols. Tokyo: Kōshaku Matsukata Masayoshi Den Hensankai, 1935.

Tōyō Keizai Shimpō (The Oriental Economist), Tokyo, 1895–1938.

Tsubotani Zenshirō, ed. Tōdai meiryū gojūka hōko roku (Fifty Talks by Famous Men of Our Times). Tokyo: Hakubunkan, 1899.

Tsuchiya Takao. Nihon no keieisha seishin (The Spirit of Japanese Management). Tokyo: Keizai Ōraisha, 1959.

——— Nihon no seishō (Japanese Political Merchants). Tokyo: Keizai Ōraisha, 1956.

——— Nihon shihon shugi no keieishiteki kenkyū (Studies in the History of Management in Japanese Capitalism). Tokyo: Misuzu Shobō, 1954.

——— Nihon shihon shugi shijō no shidōshatachi (Pioneers in the History of Japanese Capitalism). Tokyo: Iwanami Shoten, 1939.

——— Zaibatsu o kizuita hitobito (The Men Who Built the Zaibatsu). Tokyo: Kōbundo, 1955.

Tsunoda, Ryusaka, Wm. Theodore de Bary, and Donald Keene, compilers. Sources of the Japanese Tradition. New York: Columbia University Press, 1958.

Tsurumi Yūsuke, ed. Gotō Shimpei (Gotō Shimpei). 4 vols. Tokyo: Gotō Shimpei Haku Denki Hensankai, 1937–38.

Usami Shōgo. Matsunaga Yasuzaemon den (A Biography of Matsunaga Yasuzaemon). Tokyo: Tōyō Shokan, 1959.

Uzaki Kumakichi. Toyokawa Ryōhei (Toyokawa Ryōhei). Tokyo: Toyokawa Ryōhei Denki Hensankai, 1922.

Vogel, Ezra F. Japan's New Middle Class: The Salary Man and His Family in a Tokyo Suburb. Berkeley, Calif.: University of California, 1963.

Wada Tsutou. Kinbara Meizen (Kinbara Meizen). Tokyo: Nihon Shobō, 1959.

Wakamiya Unosuke. Morimura ō genkō roku (A Record of the Sayings and Deeds of Morimura Ichizaemon). Tokyo: Okura Shoten, 1929.

Walker, S. H., and Paul Sklar. Business Finds Its Voice: Management's Effort to Sell the Business Idea to the Public. New York: Harper & Bros., 1938.

Watanabe Kazuhide. Kyojin Nakajima Chikuhei (The Great Nakajima Chikuhei). Tokyo: Hōbun Shorin, 1955.

Watarai, Toshiharu. "Nationalization of Railways in Japan," in Faculty of Political Science, Studies in History, Economics and Public Law (New York: Columbia University, 1915), LXIII, 2, 189–339.

Yamaguchi Kisaburō Den Hensan Iinkai, eds. Yamaguchi Kisaburō den (A Biography of Yamaguchi Kisaburō). Tokyo: Tōkyō Shibaura Denki K.K., 1950.

Yamaji Aizan. Gendai kinken shi (A History of the Power of Money in Recent Times). Tokyo: Hatori Shoten, 1908.

Yamamoto Sanehiko. Kawasaki Shōzō (Kawasaki Shōzō). Tokyo: Yoshimatsu Sadashizu, 1918.

Yamazaki Kazuyoshi. Kuhara Fusanosuke (Kuhara Fusanosuke). Tokyo: Tōkai Shuppansha, 1939.

Yano Fumio. Yasuda Zenjirō (Yasuda Zenjirō). Tokyo: Yasuda Hōzensha, 1925.

Yano Tsuneta Kinenkai, eds. Yano Tsuneta den (A Biography of Yano Tsuneta). Tokyo: Yano Tsuneta Kinenkai, 1957.

Yasuda Gakuen Shō O Kenkyūkai, eds. Shō ō Yasuda Zenjirō den (A Biography of Yasuda Zenjirō). Tokyo: Yasuda Gakuen Shō O Kenkyūkai, 1958.

Yoshino Kōichi, ed. Zen Keinosuke tsuisōroku (Recollections of Zen Keinosuke). Tokyo: Nihon Dantai Seimei Hoken K.K., 1959.

Index

America, *see* Western world
Asabuki Eiji (1850–1918, Mitsui executive), 66, 100
Association for the Study of Social Policy, 94–96
Association of Industrial Organizations of the Kantō Region
Auyukawa Gisuke (1880–   , Nissan enterprises), 106n

Baba Eiichi (1879–1937, Kangyō Bank), 100
business ideology, 4
businessmen, and political power, 2–5, 19–20, 43n, 44, 77, 92–93, 104, 115–19, 127n, 128n, 133n; motivation of, 4, 18n, 117n, 121n; on role of government, 18–29, 52–55, 60, 62, 73–78 *passim*, 82–83, 89, 94–96, 104–12 *passim*; education of, 40, 71–72, 101; class origins of, 41n, 48, 97–98; and samurai spirit, 46–50, 76, 97–98, 102–3, 115–16. *See also individual businessmen by name*

Chambers of Commerce, *see under* Kōchi, Japan, Nagoya, Osaka, *and* Tokyo
Chisō Zōcho Kisei Dōmeikai, 45
communism, *see under* socialism
competition, in Anglo-American

ideology, 2, 31, 49, 113–14; between Japan and West, 11, 13–19 *passim*, 33, 47–50 *passim*, 55, 72–74, 88–89, 108–9; between government and private enterprise, 21–24; essential to progress, 23, 26, 32, 39, 95–96, 107; need for regulation, 25–28, 34–35, 54. *See also* cooperation *and* self-interest
Confucianism, *see under* traditional values
cooperation, essential to progress, 25, 34–35, 74; as a traditional value, 57, 60, 63–64, 76; appeal to workers for, 68, 72–73, 74, 79–84 *passim*, 95, 98; and business success, 100–101

Dan Takuma (1858–1932, Mitsui executive), on labor problems, 56–57, 66n; president of Japan Industrial Club, 80; on capitalists, 98–99; on meaning of success, 101–2; exemplifies Japanese spirit, 102–4; assassination, 104–6
Denki Kyōkai, *see under* Electric Power Association
dōgyō kumiai, 24–27, 29

education, traditional values in, 10, 32, 61, 91–92; of workers, 18,

67, 68–69, 79, 91–92, 132n, 135–36n; of businessmen, 40, 71–72, 101
Electric Power Association, 107–8
Electric Power Control Bill, 107–8
England, see Western world

Factory Act of 1911, 55n, 58. See also under government
familism (*kazoku shugi*), in Meiji business ideology, 57–64 *passim*, 73–76 *passim*; Suzuki Bunji endorses, 79; after First World War, 81–88 *passim*; concept of, 91n. See also cooperation, paternalism *and* traditional values
Federation of Filatures, 66
foreign trade, see competition
Fuji Masazumi (Kanegafuchi Spinning Co.), 74n
Fujita Densaburō (1842–1912, Osaka promoter), 37–38
Fujiwara Genjirō (1869–1960, Oji Paper Co.), 100
Fujiyama Raita (1863–1938, Fujiyama enterprises), 33, 85, 124n
Fukuda Tokuzō (1874–1930, political economist), 95
Fukuzawa Yukichi (1834–1901, Meiji intellectual), 15, 32ff, 73, 115

Gō Seinosuke (1865–1942, President of National Federation of Industrial Organizations), 102–3
Godai Tomoatsu (1834–85, Osaka promoter), 19, 36, 42
Gotō Shimpei (1857–1929, government official), 72
government, commitment to industrialization, 14–15, 16–18; ownership of enterprises, 17–18, 20–24, 106–7; regulation of business, 24–29, 104–12; intervention in labor relations, 52–55, 60–62, 73–76, 82, 94–96; suppression of labor unions, 78, 83, 89. See also politics

Hara Rokurō (1844–1923, banker), 42, 48, 127n
harmony, see cooperation

Hatano Shōgorō (1854–1929, Mitsui executive), 40–41, 42n
Hatano Tsurukichi (1858–1918, Gunze Silk Co.), 36–37
Hibiya Heizaemon (1849–1921, Kanegafuchi Spinning Co.), 74
Hirao Hachisaburō (1866–1945, Kawasaki Shipping Co.), 71, 103
Hirose Saihei (1828–1914, Sumitomo executive), 54n, 71

Ikeda Seihin (1857–1950, Mitsui executive), 98n, 110
Ikeo Yoshizō (President of Electric Power Association), 107–8
individualism: in Anglo-American ideology, 2, 30–31, 113; rejection of in Japan, 3ff, 33ff, 50, 77ff, 85, 92, 96–97, 114, 119. See also competition *and* self-interest
Inoue Kaoru (1835–1915, Meiji statesman), 10, 127n
Inoue Shōzō (1848–86, government official), 15–16
Inukai Tsuyoshi (1855–1932, political leader), 47–48
Itō Hirobumi (1841–1909, Meiji statesman), 62
Iwasaki Yatarō (1834–85, Mitsubishi enterprises), 132n, 137n

Japan Chamber of Commerce, 85
Japan Cotton Spinners Association (Nihon Menshi Bōseki Dōgyō Rengōkai), 66
Japan Economic Federation (Nihon Keizai Renmeikai), 108, 110
Japan Industrial Club (Nihon Kōgyō Kurabu), 80–89 *passim*

Kanai Noboru (1865–1933, political economist), 95
Kanegafuchi Spinning Mills, 66–67, 74
Kaneko Kentarō (1853–1942, government official), 42, 55
Kangyō Shimonkai (Councils for the Promotion of Industry), 27, 53
Kantō Sangyō Dantai Rengōkai, 88
Kinbara Meizen (1832–1923, industrial promoter), 35, 48–49

Kiyoura Keigo (1850–1942, statesman), 80–81
Kōchi Chamber of Commerce, 20n
Kuhara Fusanosuke (1869–195?, Kuhara enterprises), 99, 106n, 107
Kuroda Kiyotaka (1840–1900, Meiji statesman), 15n
Kuwada Kumazō (1868–1932, political economist), 95–96
Kyōchōkai, 81–84, 86, 96–97, 101–2
Kyōdō Un'yū Kaisha (United Transportation Co.), 27

labor class, *see* workers
labor legislation, *see under* government
labor unions, 7, 78–79, 83, 89
laissez-faire, 13–29 *passim*; 32–33. See also competition, government, *and* individualism

Major Industries Association Ordinance of 1941, 111
Makino Motojirō (banker), 103
Marxism, *see* socialism
Matsukata Kōjirō (1865–1950, Kawasaki Shipping Co.) 41–42, 43
Matsukata Masayoshi (1835–1924, Meiji statesman), 21–22, 37
Matsunaga Yasuzaemon (1875– , electric power industry), 106–7
Meiji Restoration, 9–12
Minomura Rizaemon (1821–77, Mitsui enterprises), 19, 25
Mitsubishi enterprises, 22–23, 27–28, 69, 103. See also *individual executives by name*
Mitsui enterprises, 98, 103f, 110. See also *individual executives by name*
Morimura Ichizaemon (1839–1919, export trade), 25, 35ff, 49
Motoori Norinaga (18th century moralist), 7
Muro Kyūsō (1858–1934, Confucian scholar), 7–8
Mutō Sanji (1867–1934, Kanegafuchi Spinning Co.), 66, 86–88, 98

Nagoya Chamber of Commerce, 19, 22, 58, 60, 73–74

Nakahashi Tokugorō (1864–1934, Osaka Shipping Co.), 72–73
Nakamigawa Hikojirō (1854–1901, Mitsui enterprises), 137n
National Federation of Industrial Organizations (Zenkoku Sangyō Dantai Rengōkai), 89
Natsume Sōseki (1867–1912, Meiji Novelist), 40
Nihon Keizai Renmeikai (Japan Economic Federation), 108, 110
Nihon Kōgyō Kurabu (Japan Industrial Club), 80–89 *passim*
Nihon Menshi Bōseki Dōgyō Rengōkai (Japan Cotton Spinners' Association), 66
Ninomiya Sontoku (19th century moralist), 70–71
Nishimura Shigeki (Meiji intellectual), 11

Ogura Masatane (Sumitomo executive), 132n
Oji Paper Company, 64n, 100
Okubo Toshimichi (1830–78, Meiji statesman), 15n, 16–17, 17n
Okuma Shigenobu (1838–1922, political leader), 23, 80
Okura Kihachirō (1835–1928, Okura enterprises), 17n, 27–28, 46, 47, 52, 59, 73
Osaka Chamber of Commerce, 20–25 *passim*
oyakata (labor subcontractor), 68–69

paternalism, 60–69, 81–83, 87–91, 116. See also cooperation, familism, *and* traditional values
patriotism, *see* service
Peace Preservation Law, of 1900, 83; of 1925, 107n
political power, and the business class, 2–5, 19–20, 43n, 44, 47, 77, 92–93, 104, 115–19, 127–28n, 133n; and democracy, 4–5, 77, 117–19; and the military, 5–6, 104–11 *passim*, 119
private property, 23, 75, 95, 107n. See also self-interest *and* wealth
profits, 8, 23, 36, 40–41, 108–9, 111. See also self-interest

samurai, as social elite, 5–9; and
businessmen, 41n, 46–50, 76, 97–
98, 102–3, 115–16
Seishi Dōmei, 66
self-interest, eschewal by businessmen, 3, 31, 34–43, 78, 101–3,
114–18 *passim*; businessmen condemned for pursuing, 7, 10–11,
24–25, 92, 101–4 *passim*, 109;
incentive to effort, 30–33, 38–40,
95–96, 108ff, 113, 117–18; and
labor relations, 54, 59, 70, 76, 81–
89 *passim*, 97–98. *See also* competition *and* individualism
Senjū Woolen Mills, 15, 17
service, as goal of business, 3, 31,
34–43, 46–49, 70–71, 99, 101–3,
116–17; as samurai ideal, 6, 8–9,
46–49; and self-sacrifice, 34–41;
and appeals to workers, 58, 70–
71, 74, 91–92, 116
Shibaura Electric Works, 69
Shibusawa Eiichi (1840–1931,
banker), on self-interest, 3, 34–
35, 39–40; condemns merchants,
10; on role of government, 22,
25ff; on service to society, 38–40;
on success, 38–40, 71–72; on political power, 45; on labor problems, 54n, 56, 64n, 78–79, 81–84
Shimada Saburō (1852–1923,
political leader), 23
Shōda Heigorō (1847–1922, Mitsubishi enterprises), 23, 28, 75–76
Smith, Adam, 30
social mobility, 6, 98, 100, 123n.
See also success
socialism, in Meiji Japan, 61–62,
95–96; after First World War,
78, 80, 92, 96–97, 107n, 118,
136n; Suzuki Bunji on Marxism,
79; businessmen on Marxist
unions, 92, 105; Kyōchōkai on,
96–97; Kuhara Fusanosuke on
communism, 107
Soeda Juichi (1864–1929, government official), 58–59, 78, 129n
spiritual compensation, 96–97, 101–
2, 126n
success, and patriotic motivation,
35–38; secret to, 36–37, 70–73,
99–101; wealth as measure of,

46, 114–15. *See also* self-interest
and service
Sumitomo, 54n, 71, 103
Suzuki Bunji (1885–1946, labor
leader), 78–79
Suzuki Tōsaburō (1855–1913,
sugar industry), 36, 70

Taguchi Ukichi (Meiji intellectual), 32–33
Tamura Masanori (Shimano Spinning Mills), 58, 60, 67–68
Tokyo Chamber of Commerce, 22,
26, 52–53, 56ff
traditional values, and pursuit of
profit, 2–12 *passim*, 19, 32, 34,
38–40, 45–47, 106, 114–15; in
education, 10, 41, 61, 91; in labor
relations, 52–64 *passim*, 70–71,
75–76, 81–89 *passim*; contrasted
with Western capitalism, 62, 66n,
79–92 *passim*, 102–3, 109, 116
Tsuda Shingo (1884–1948, Kanegafuchi Spinning Co.), 99, 107

Versailles Peace Treaty, 86f

Wada Gakikenzō (1860–1919,
political economist), 95
Washington Conference of 1919, 86
wealth, 33, 49, 112, 115. *See also*
profits *and* self-interest
Western world, business ideology
in, 1–2, 30–32, 49, 75, 99, 112–
15 *passim*; competition between
Japan and, 11–16 *passim*, 33, 47–
50 *passim*, 55, 72–74, 88–89,
108–9; as model for industrialization, 14–21, *passim*, 25–26, 29,
33–34; as model for labor legislation, 51–62 *passim*, 66n, 80–
84 *passim*, 95–96; values of contrasted with Japanese spirit, 57–
62 *passim*, 79–92 *passim*, 102–3,
108. *See also* individualism *and*
laissez-faire
work, as a moral value, 97; as secret
to success, 100
Workers, shortage of skilled, 52, 59,
65–69; in factories, 64–65, 90–
91, 135n; village background of,
63–64, 91; education of, 68–69,

79, 91–92, 132n, 135n; distinction between types, 70n; opportunity for upward mobility, 98, 100

Yamaga Sokō (17th century moralist), 5–6
Yamagata Aritomo (1838–1922, government leader), 10–11
Yamaguchi Kisaburō (1874–1947, Furukawa enterprises), 67–68
Yano Tsuneta (1865–1954, Daiichi Life Insurance), 106

Yasuda Zenjirō (1838–1921, Yasuda enterprises), 71
Yūaikai (The Friendly Society), 78–79

zaibatsu, 67, 76, 99, 104, 106n, 111. *See also* Mitsubishi, Mitsui, Sumitomo, *and* Yasuda
Zen Keinosuke (1887–1951, Insurance executive), 102
Zenkoku Sangyō Dantai Rengōkai (National Federation of Industrial Organizations), 89